# HISTORY'S GREATEST DECEPTIONS AND CONFIDENCE SCAMS

Steven Lazaroff & Mark Rodger

RodgerLaz Publishing S.E.N.C.
www.Rodgerlaz.com

Ordering Information:
Quantity sales. Special discounts are available on quantity purchases by corporations, associations, and others. For details, contact the publisher at the address above.
Orders by U.S. trade bookstores and wholesalers. Please contact the publisher at the address above or by email: slazaroff@rodgerlaz.com

Printed in Canada

Publisher's Cataloging-in-Publication data
Steven Lazaroff and Mark Rodger.
History's greatest deceptions and confidence scams / Mark Rodger and Steven Lazaroff.
p. cm.
ISBN 978-1-7752921-2-8
1. The main category of the book —History —Other category. 2. Confidence tricks and scams.

First Edition

14 13 12 11 10 / 10 9 8 7 6 5 4 3 2 1

# DEDICATION

Steven Lazaroff - Dedicated to my wife, Natasha, the love of my life.

Mark Rodger - Dedicated to all the swindlers, con men and smooth-talking salesmen out there that dream big and think fast.

# Other works by the authors

A Question of Time – Steven Lazaroff

History's Greatest Missing Treasures – Mark Rodger

Where Are They? And Why Haven't We Found Them Yet?
– Steven Lazaroff, Mark Rodger

The Chronicles of Talwin – Steven Lazaroff

# CONTENTS

# ACKNOWLEDGEMENTS

We would like to acknowledge several people.

First, that eternal rascal the con artist. May they continue to dream up a method to part a fool from his or her money.

To Clive Armstrong, our high school English teacher.

To R.J. Lynch, our editor and an author in his own right, a true gentleman and a perfectionist.

To the people instrumental with the production of this book. Natasha, who spent hours on formatting. Our collaborators Charles Hill and Nicky Hoseck, and the wonderful background research done by Jeffrey R Coffey. You all have our eternal gratitude.

To our family and friends who read what we were putting out, and for all their feedback.

"NEVER ATTEMPT TO WIN BY FORCE WHAT
CAN BE WON BY DECEPTION."

—   Niccolò Machiavelli, The Prince

This book was written using UK English

# THE TEN COMMANDMENTS OF CONFIDENCE ARTISTS

- Be a patient listener

- Never look bored

- Wait for the other person to reveal any political opinions, and then agree with them

- Let the other person reveal religious views, and then have the same ones.

- Hint at sex talk, but don't follow it up unless the other person shows a strong interest.

- Never discuss illness, unless some special concern is shown.

- Never pry into a person's personal circumstances; they'll tell you all eventually.

- Never boast - just let your importance be quietly obvious.

- Never be untidy.

- Never get drunk.

# INTRODUCTION

The term "scam" is really a new word in the English lexicon and has come to supersede its older and more distinguished original cousin, "the confidence game" or "con game", as it became popularly known at the time. One constant in human history is the tendency to want to shorten and simplify some of the most descriptive concepts we have, to anything that can be mumbled as a single syllable mouthful.

Throughout history, there have always been fraudsters and tricksters ready and willing to part people from their money with smooth-talking and tall tales, but the first formally recorded "confidence trick" was uniquely American in its origins and set the bar for both simplicity and sheer guts, both hallmarks of the most successful frauds ever perpetrated.

In the late 1840s, the east coast of the United States was awash with the nouveau riche, and men wearing top hats to look important. Good manners and polite society were everything unless you were a slave in which case the top hat was entirely optional. It was the age of Jane Austen, white gloves, carriages and over-the-top manners. It was also the time of pocket watches, dangling from gold chains. Victorian sensibilities dictated that the bigger and shinier the watch, the bigger and shinier the man.

Enter one William Thompson, arguably the originator of the term "confidence man", a genius operator and a personal hero to the career grifter. Little is known about where he came from, but what is certain is that he had his finger on the pulse of well-heeled suckers strolling the walkways and avenues of Manhattan in the mid-nineteenth century.

Meeting someone was a rigid, formal affair with protocol and procedures; the handshake, tip of the hat and bow were rigidly choreographed. Failure to introduce oneself properly or be introduced according to accepted custom was seen as an embarrassment to both parties – and embarrassment was worse than a bleeding head wound, to be avoided at all costs. Operating in New York in the 1840s, William was a keen observer of human behaviour. He realized that, with such pomp and ceremony surrounding every introduction, it was considered the ultimate in bad manners not to remember people that one might have been acquainted with – he calculated that when confronted with a stranger that said he was a friend, most men would likely act as though they remembered a meeting that had never happened.

William thought he might be able to leverage this, and so would often stroll along the city streets, until he spotted an upper-class sucker, at which time he would approach and pretend to know them and be a past acquaintance, someone that they had met before. Rather than be embarrassed, the mark would usually smile, nod and pretend that he knew who William was – better that than risk dishonour, or a pistol duel – which was how some matters of honour were settled at the time.

After some friendly chatting, and a little trust-gaining, Thompson would throw out his hook, asking "Have you confidence in me to trust me with your watch until tomorrow?" He wasn't all about watches – sometimes he would ask for money. It's good to diversify. More often than not, the mark would part with the watch or the money (or sometimes both), and William would depart, promising to meet the next day to return the property. Naturally, he didn't keep the next day's appointment and would often stroll away, laughing to himself.

He repeated this game dozens of times until he had the bad luck to happen across a former victim, who promptly summoned a roving policeman who gave chase. After a frantic foot pursuit through Manhattan and a dramatic struggle, William was bodily subdued and arrested. Perhaps he was slowed down by the weight of all those pocket watches; it was reported that he had several on him at the time he was caught.

His arrest and the subsequent article in the New York Herald called "Arrest of the Confidence Man" made headlines across the country; he was headed to trial in 1849. The press noted his specific appeals to victims' "confidence", and thereafter he was known in the press as "The Confidence Man". And so the term was born, and "confidence game" or "con" became part of our vocabulary, and spawned an endless series of quick-buck fraudster copycats that said, "me too"!

This is the story of some of the greatest.

# EGYPTIAN ANIMAL MUMMY FAKERY

The culture of the ancient Egyptians is fascinating for many
reasons, and one wonders if they knew how much their pyramids would
contribute to the tourism industry centuries later. They loved building,
making mummies and decorating everything with hieroglyphs, particularly
of dogs, birds, the occasional eye symbol and lots and lots of cats. The
Egyptians viewed animals as sacred beings and affiliated them to the gods;
two out of every five hieroglyphs discovered contain some sort of animal
artwork and writing.

Central to daily life in Egypt was the worship of many, many gods in
a complex religious system where deities and demigods controlled the
forces of nature, impacted all aspects of the day and loomed large when it
came to the afterlife. A people eager to gain favour with their gods evolved
complex rituals, ceremonies and sacrifices; even the most primitive human

culture has always appreciated that it's better to have a god happy with you than unhappy.

Egyptian art offers splendid examples of how the ancients understood their gods' mythological roles and manifestations, and how they imagined they might look like a person; animal/human hybrids were common. The god Horus was often represented by falcons, a mongoose or a shrew, Anubis by jackals or dogs, and cats were closely associated with the goddess Bastet, particularly important to childbearing women. Often several animals represented the same god, or several gods could be incarnated as the same animal. The god Thoth was often pictured as a baboon, at other times as an ibis bird; the gods Mat, Hathor and Bastet could be all be a lioness, the god Atum could be a lizard, a snake or an eel. Even after the country was eventually unified, there was generally no real standard for a uniting gospel or centralised church dogma – giving birth to many different variations. Certainly, to the ancient tourist, it must have been a pretty confusing system, but to the ancient Egyptians, it was serious business. Before 3000 B.C., animals were not themselves worshipped as gods, but they were seen as possible ambassadors of them. Best to be respected and honoured; you never knew when your local god would send a blessing or favour through a neighbourhood pet, and any beast might be the incarnation of a powerful god, just hanging around; it was better to be safe than sorry when it came to respecting the Divine or their agents. In fact, a general theme in religious teachings at the time dictated that, once a person's life ended, they would have to go through a series of judgment questions and their acceptance into or banishment from the afterlife would depend on how well or how poorly they treated animals. Yes, it was a good time to be a house cat.

During this time, the wanton killing of animals was a capital offence. One Greek historian wrote that he once witnessed the lynching of a Roman merchant who accidentally killed a cat while visiting Egypt. No doubt slaves at the time wished they had that kind of respect.

When one thinks of ancient Egypt, the images of pyramids and mummies are invariably intertwined. The practice of Egyptian mummification has been a fascinating one for generations around the world with archaeologists, scientists, historians, and gifted amateur Egyptologists delving deep into Egyptian culture to demystify and decode it for the rest of the world.

While many theories and hypotheses have come and gone, one thing has been consistent and clear - the Egyptians believed that animals were sacred. And this is why they slaughtered and mummified them in huge numbers.

Before wholesale animal mummification became a national industry, religious pilgrims and the believers seeking to pay homage at the local sacred temple would offer animal statuettes made of bronze to find favour from or appease their gods – and they were ready to pay good coin for them.

As a finishing flourish, black paint was used to draw on life-like features, and a fashionable eye adornment was coloured glass, rock crystals or obsidian. Hand-crafted or moulded, these took significant time to create and complete expertly. A cheaper and faster alternative would be found – like making a mummy of the real animal instead.

Particularly popular, cat mummies were in high demand. The mummy makers would usually strangle the cats or break their necks to end their lives, afterwards drying out the organs and filling the bodies with soil; their limbs would be wrapped and positioned in such a way that they were either in a sitting position or close to their bodies. Pieces of fabric were then tied around the cats using intricate geometric patterns. The finished felines were then placed for eternity in either wooden or bronze sarcophagi, usually highly decorated and still expensive, but certainly a lot easier than commissioning a metal one.

As large-scale production became more necessary, the process became more simplified and faster. Human mummification ensured that all body parts were dried but present, unlike animal mummies that were filled with either sand or clothing or whatever happened to be on hand at the back of the store. Producers dipped the animals in resin, tied them with coarse linen and called it a day; human mummy creators treated their charges with an exotic variety of products - petroleum bitumen, coniferous cedar resin, sugar gum, beeswax, special oils and fats to name a few. Faster and cheaper – that was the way to do it when it came to sending the beloved animal into the afterlife.

Adapting to the sacrifice and preservation of the real thing, the Egyptians came to believe that they were honouring not just the animal, but also the god the animal represented. By having animal totems ritually killed and then mummifying the remains either to leave as an offering or to place in a catacomb alongside their own mummy when their time came, they were sending a message to the afterlife. Arguably the Kardashians of their time, the Theban queen Makare and her half-sister Sekhmet were entombed with a green pet monkey and pet gazelle respectively; Princes Tuthmosis and Hapymen were found to be accompanied into the afterlife by mummified pet cats and dogs. Ibis birds had a particularly rough time and were rendered near-extinct along with many other species. A 2015 research project using radiocarbon dating demonstrated a dramatic increase in bird mummies entombed during the Ptolemaic period, notable for being the time of Cleopatra and Alexander the Great. Pet mummification was big business, practised by both the affluent and ordinary Egyptians alike, and – just like today – if the rich and powerful were doing it, everyone else wanted to do it too. The industry became so lucrative that it attracted professional craftspeople including embalmers, animal keepers, priests and catacomb and cemetery builders.

Different cults across Egypt worshipped animals as a vessel for their gods, further fuelling demand. The followers would choose a particular animal as a totem and care for it lavishly until it died of natural causes after which they would mummify the "chosen" animal and then choose another as a successor and continue the cycle.

The cult of the Apis Bull is a particularly good example and started operating as early as 800 B.C. Representing gods such as Osiris and Ptah, a chosen bull would spend its life in the comfort of a lavish temple, pampered with hand massages, choice foodstuffs and lots and lots of chanting and praise. Reportedly devotees would observe the bull's movements, moods and even excrement trying to interpret what message was being sent by the Divine concerned. The beast was allowed to die naturally; unless it reached the age of 28 years old at which time it was killed, the cultists probably having run out of patience by then. After it died, there would follow elaborate mourning ceremonies and a splendid funeral procession. Bull mummification would follow, and extra-large, purpose-built tables complete with drainage channels for fluids were used for the embalming, such as have been found in the city of Memphis. After the preservation process was finished, bull mummy makers would wrap the animal in linen and then add artificial eyes to complete the "natural" look.

Similar was the cult of the crocodile, commonly representing gods of fertility and the sun. At the Shedet temple also known as Crocodilopolis, crocodile mummies were lined up in the temple, and Egyptians often carried them in precession during ceremonies. Pampered throughout most of their lifetimes, the crocodiles were often mummified using gold and other precious metals. With time, mummy creators became so busy with orders that they stopped giving crocodiles the lavish treatments and settled for faster, more practical ways.

Beast mummification went beyond the vagaries of the religious; household pets and beloved animals were preserved and mummified to keep the animals close to their masters even after death, protecting the animal's immortality. Animals like gazelles, birds, dogs, mongoose mongooses, monkeys, and cats were among the favourites, and it was common practice to inscribe the master's favourite pet on his tomb upon demise. Archaeologists have discovered a multitude of mummy inscriptions depicting over 70 unique pet names. Oddly, pigs and hippos do not appear in the archaeological record. It seems that there wasn't any interest in mummifying them or perhaps they weren't really a popular choice as "household companion".

Over 30 burial sites for mummified animals have been identified, and some historians believe that more than 70 million animals were entombed in Saqqara, Beni Hassan, Bubastis, and Thebes; sites are estimated to hold millions of specimens. At Tune-el-Gebel, excavations have revealed more than 4 million ibis bird mummies, and it is determined that the Saqqara burial site alone saw an estimated 10,000 ibis bird offerings each year according to the best data available.

All this demand for animal murder and ritualistic preservation drastically impacted the candidates available for mummification, and there is clear evidence that falcons, baboons, ibis birds, hawks, cats, dogs and many other species were pushed to the brink of extinction. Animal breeding programmes sprouted in temples and small villages near the temples to keep up with demand. Sacrificial demand had become so rampant that there was simply no more readily and easily obtainable supply of animals anymore. The more exotic and powerful the god one was looking to sacrifice to, the rarer and strange the animal had to be, and this led to a rise in mummy forgeries.

Towards the end of the 19th century, the British Government shipped over 19 tonnes of mummified cats discovered at Saqqara out of the country, much of it to be used as fertiliser by farmers while the balance was sent to the British Museum of Natural Sciences. The Museum director, a one Dr Morrison-Scott started a meticulous examination of the remains and discovered that the cat mummification was not as expert as Egyptologists had first thought, but rather a haphazard stuffing of the cats with random body parts. In some of the cat mummies he found no animal parts at all, but an assortment of twigs, rocks and in some cases scraps of clothing.

Recent research in the UK has revealed that the entire industry was rife with slapdash animal mummies that might indicate large scale, industrial fraud. Using cutting-edge medical imaging technology, they found that a significant number contained either partial or no animal remains at all. A collaborative team of researchers from the University of Manchester and the Manchester Museum examined and analysed over 800 animal specimens found in mummies in the most extensive study ever conducted into the subject, comprising Egyptologists, radiographers and researchers. They used X-ray and CT scanning equipment to scan through the protective wrappings of animals preservations that originated from Egypt in the 19th and 20th century. Hoping to shed some light on the condition of the remains and gather a better understanding of the mummification process, the researchers scanned an assortment of mummies expecting to find animals like cats, birds, shrews and a Nile crocodile that was five feet long.

The findings baffled many - the mummy that supposedly contained a five-foot crocodile had eight baby crocodiles; a cat mummy consisted only of cat bones, which was unexpected because the mummy itself had been crafted to show all the external features of a cat such as a nose, paws and even tiny ears. Only a third of the mummies examined contained complete animal remains. The other third contained partial remains, while the final percentage batch contained no animal remains at all - the mummy creators had stuffed the mummies only with linen, mud, sticks and other material. After all, who would bother unwrapping the finished product? Sacrilege!

The findings have caused hot debate, with experts around the world wondering if ancient embalmers took advantage of unsuspecting victims and sold fraudulent mummies, but charged top prices as if for the real, crafted product. Some experts believe it was probably known at the time that embalmers were taking shortcuts, or only providing part of the animal within the mummy in the belief that in the afterlife a portion of the beast would magically become the whole; what may have mattered most to the Egyptians was the mummy's exterior rather than the interior. It must have been known at the time that forgeries were common in the ancient Egyptian marketplace, given that stock of the real article became harder and harder to procure.

This could certainly have been a plausible explanation, given that the sample size of "fake" animal mummies discovered was small in comparison to the number of complete specimens that were found, but recent studies have suggested a booming industry in animal mummies where forgeries far outnumbered the genuine article – some would call it a fraud of epic proportions.

Recent excavations at Saqquara by Selima Ikram, a distinguished Egyptology professor, and a team of international researchers uncovered roughly eight million mummified animals in a catacomb dedicated to Anubis – God of the Underworld and Death represented almost exclusively by dogs or dog-life figures. However, the large sample of animal remains present were not purely canine at all, but an assortment of dogs, mongooses, and cats and even some birds, most wrapped to represent a dog mummy.

On a different excavation, in a catacomb in Southern Cairo next to the Temple of Anubis, the magnitude of the catacombs was shocking – supposed dog mummies were stacked between 1.2 and 1.5 meters high. More than 2500 years old, archaeologists estimate that it contains roughly 7.8 million mummified animal remains. Even with breeding programs functioning like ancient puppy mills it would be impossible to provide so vast a quantity of dogs for sacrificial purposes.

Far more probable is that, as demand increased for animals to be sent on that eternal journey, supply probably shrank, despite any attempt by enterprising ancient breeding programs, especially for the more exotic candidates like baboons and crocodiles. The shortfall was likely made up by making economies – parts of the whole animal rather than the whole, the better to stretch the supply. It would be doubtful that any discounts were offered to reflect that only a percentage of the expected animals were actually in the final package. What naturally follows is that, since no one was unwrapping the merchandise to inspect the finished product anyway, a steady stream of forgeries made their way into temples, shrines and catacombs while the makers continued to make as much money as they could get away with – just as happens today. Greed has always has been consistent, and the manufacture and sale of the vast amount of fraudulent animal mummies that must be still out there, represented and then sold as the real thing, must rank as one of the biggest scams in human history.

# CONSTANTINE THE GREAT

The phrase "if you can't beat them, join them" comes to mind when considering the illustrious career of Flavius Valerius Aurelius Constantinus Augustus – or Constantine the Great as history came to know him. Raised a pagan, and practiced in the art of murder, fraud and the age-old Roman tradition of killing your own family members, Constantine succeeded in reinventing himself as a great Christian and patron of the church; so much so that this 57th Emperor of the Roman Empire was eventually canonized as a Saint by the Eastern Orthodox, Oriental Orthodox, Eastern Catholic and some branches of the Lutheran Churches. History it seems can actually have a very short memory.

Constantine the Great had a remarkable reign of 31 years, second in length only to the very first Roman Emperor Octavian Augustus. He is remembered for one specific aspect that changed the course of the spiritual world, and world history for that matter; Constantine, in his late-night visions and wildest self-aggrandising fantasies couldn't predict what he would achieve - he was the first Roman Emperor to accept the Christian faith. Or did he?

Granting Christians the right to practice their religion openly, he stopped their persecutions and exterminations and returned confiscated properties (or those not already in the hands of his friends and supporters) to their former Christian owners. The official establishment of Christianity as the state religion would have to wait for another emperor, Theodosius, in 380 A.D.

He who would be the Roman Emperor Constantine came into the world around 272 A.D. and was the son of a military officer and a woman of low social standing named Helen. It is uncertain if Constantine was legitimate, as there is no evidence that his father and Helen were actually married. In all likelihood, she was his concubine or a prostitute who had achieved a little legitimacy. Born Flavius Valerius Constantinus, it is reported that even as a child he was destined for a greater purpose than his peers, having that "special something"; considering that Constantine himself practically wrote his own biographies this isn't really surprising. It's incredible how good you can make yourself look when you're writing your own version of history.

Constantine's father was Flavius Constantius who hailed from Illyricum, a province located in the Eastern half of the Roman Empire. When another Illyrian became the new Emperor Aurelian, he took all his drinking buddies along for the Imperial ride, and Flavius achieved some success as one of the new Emperor's bodyguards. Roman rulers were notoriously short-lived, and after a brief time at the top, the unfortunate Aurelian was murdered by his own elite Praetorian guards.

Romans had a time-honoured tradition of military service as a stepping stone to eventual political office, and when another Illyrian companion of Aurelian's named Diocletian was elevated to the office of Emperor, he appointed Flavius as Governor of the Roman province of Dalmatia. Diocletian thought that the empire was too vast for any one man to rule effectively, so in 285 A.D. he made reforms in the Imperial system and appointed another Illyrian comrade named Maximian as his co-Emperor in the Western half of the empire, the better to share duties. Each Emperor would have his own court, military and administrative faculties and also a deputy emperor to assist in holding it all together. In 293 A.D. Constantine's father was promoted by Maximian as the deputy emperor in the west, while young Constantine was sent east where he could gain an education in Diocletian's court and live as his father's heir presumptive – it was expected that he would take over from Constantinus when the time came. Actually, he was more of a hostage to ensure Flavius stayed on his best behaviour. Although they liked to flock together, it seems that Illyrians preferred not to trust each other too much if there was an alternative.

The ambitious young Constantine rose through the ranks of the legions until he reached the rank of tribune. A senior military officer with a distinguished service record battling barbarians and Persians until the year 303 A.D. when he returned west to the Imperial court just in time to witness the last great recorded persecution of early Christians – aptly named

"The Great Persecution". A series of edicts or Imperial orders followed against those of the Christian faith, designed to officially curtail rights, freedoms and lives. Constantine was there to see it all.

Christians would describe Diocletian's campaign as a bloodbath, and although they probably exaggerated, they claimed as many as 17,000 believers were ritually executed in just thirty days. An illegal religion in the eyes of the Roman state, Christianity and its practitioners were seen as a secretive cult, communicating in secret codes and strange, unfamiliar rituals with an irrational belief in just one god. To traditional Romans, these early Christians were challenging to understand, rejecting pagan public festivals and loudly critical of ancient, established traditions that went back for generations. Denounced as subversive to the government and the very fabric of Roman society, it was rumoured that they practised cannibalism, incest and black demonic magic as they sought to spread their religion and convert the pagan majority of the Empire. As with all social reformers, they were met with resistance by defenders of the old order who tried to hold back change, usually with a measure of violence.

Emperor Diocletian himself wanted his edicts persecuting Christians to be "without bloodshed". He ordered that they be banned from assembling in groups for worship, that their private property be confiscated, their scriptures destroyed, and their newly built Christian church at Nicomedia burned. Across the Empire, and notably in the East, the houses of Christian worship were systematically razed. Deprived of their legal rights in courts, Christians could now be legally tortured, and any believers who had achieved political or military rank lost it. For good measure,

Christians who had been freed from slavery were stripped of their free status and re-enslaved. Free to enforce capital punishment when it suited them, local judges and officials began commonly ordering that Christians be publically burned alive in something like a carnival atmosphere that was fun for the whole pagan family. Later edicts during the Persecution saw the wholesale arrest of bishops, priests, deacons and lectors; prisons swelled to bursting, with many common criminals released to make room.

During the first fifteen years of his rule, Diocletian was surrounded by virulent, public opponents of Christianity, an anti-Christian clique of counsellors that urged and supported a series of edicts against Christianity that was progressively restrictive, oppressive and brutal. Well into the 21st century, he is remembered in the Eastern Christian church as "the adversary of God".

As a close member of the Imperial court, Constantine was present for the worst excesses and most likely saw it all and participated, particularly when he accompanied Diocletian on his travels through the East Empire, where the persecutions were more vicious than in the western half of the Roman world. As Diocletian grew more suspicious and paranoid, he ordered all members of his court to make sacrifices to the old gods and directed the military to do likewise publically or lose all rank and pension and face immediate discharge. Constantine would have sworn loyalty to Jupiter, Mars and the rest of the old Roman pantheon, most likely enthusiastically, rather than earn the displeasure or wrath of the Emperor and his close supporters. As a virtual hostage, he was well aware of his delicate position as leverage against his distant father and would have taken every opportunity to ingratiate himself and be on his best behaviour. All that would change two years after he returned to Diocletian's side. The year was 305 A.D.

Sick and weakening during the winter, Diocletian publicly announced his resignation as Emperor in the east, the first in Roman history to step down voluntarily rather than being helped along the way by assassination. Strangely, his co-Emperor Maximian also resigned in the west at the same time. It was rumoured that Diocletian's deputy Galerius was really behind the push for a change in leadership to manipulate events to elevate himself to a higher position. It was commonly believed that the current deputies Galerius and Constantine's father Constantius would move up as senior Emperors and that Constantine and Maxentius (Maximian's son) would be appointed as the new deputies – family bloodlines were still expected to count for something, after all. However, Maxentius and Constantine were wholly ignored and left out in the cold. Instead, two close supporters of Galerius were proclaimed as the junior emperors – Valerius Severus (another Illyrian, and old drinking companion of Galerius) and Galerius's nephew, Maximinus Daia. Perhaps family blood wasn't utterly inconsequential after all.

At the court of Galerius (reportedly a vicious, rabid anti-Christian brute often referred to "the great Christian persecutor") Constantine knew he was in deep trouble and ancient sources report several attempts that the new senior emperor made on his life in the months following Diocletian's abdication. Recognising that his days were numbered, Constantine fled the Imperial court after a night of heavy drinking with Galerius, convincing him to allow Constantine to go west to join his father in Gaul (present-day France). Later in life, Constantine's self-proclaiming propaganda would make a minor legend of the event, detailing a dramatic escape and flight across the empire before Galerius could sober up and stop him.

Constantius didn't live long after his son joined him, dying on campaign in 306 A.D, but not before proclaiming Constantine as his heir and the new senior Emperor in the western empire, as did the soldiers of his father's army, which was certainly wonderful for him. In Imperial Roman politics, it was always better to have your endorsement for public office backed up by thousands of trained professional killers on your payroll; naturally, Constantine enthusiastically accepted. Galerius was furious but offered a compromise promotion to deputy Emperor in the West and the elevation of Valerius Severus to the senior Emperor position. Realising that this was a route to legitimacy, Constantine accepted the offer and began the process of paving the way to take over the whole empire, both east and west. Christianity and their followers provided him with a unique opportunity to forge a path to the throne.

Along with the usual civic improvements, building new monuments, and defeating aggressive barbarian tribes along the frontiers, the new deputy Caesar saw an immediate opportunity to distinguish and separate himself from Galerius "the great persecutor" and his Illyrian cohorts. He declared a formal end to the Christian persecution and all the property that had been confiscated to be returned to demonstrate his compassion, mercy and understanding. At the same time, he ordered that two captured barbarian kings and their soldiers be "fed to beasts" in the arena as part of the public celebration. Compassion, it seemed, didn't apply to everyone and Constantine began to portray himself as the possible liberator of oppressed Christians everywhere.

Almost immediately there were challenges to his position in the west from the champions of the old order, and beginning in 306 A.D. Constantine managed to isolate politically and ignore both Maximian and his son Maxentius when they took turns declaring themselves as the western Emperor and resisted his authority. In 310 A.D. Maximian went too far when while leading a portion of the army of the west – declaring Constantine dead and himself as the new Emperor and offering a sizable bribe to soldiers who would support him. It didn't work. He was eventually captured by Constantine's supporters where he was rebuked, stripped of his titles and offered clemency and forgiveness. Privately, he encouraged the former Emperor to commit suicide to avoid paying for his murder. In July of that year, Maximian obliged and hanged himself.

At first, Constantine portrayed the death as an unfortunate family tragedy – a troubled end for a troubled, dispossessed and retired Emperor. Within the year, he had changed the narrative to suit another version. The new story that he spread was that after pardoning him so graciously, Maximian plotted to murder him in his bed. Caught, he was offered the option of suicide and accepted. The new version allowed him to condemn and erase Maximian from history; Constantine ordered that all public inscriptions bearing Maximian's name and all statues bearing his likeness be destroyed. It was another example of the new western Emperor rewriting history to suit his tastes.

Understandably, Maxentius wasn't happy with his father's fate. Forgetting earlier father and son conflicts, he portrayed himself as a devoted son and proclaimed that he would seek revenge. The stage was set for a showdown in Italy and Constantine's "great transformation" into The World's Greatest Christian. Perhaps.

In the year 312 A.D., the forces of Maxentius and Constantine fought a decisive battle at the Milvian Bridge, just over the Tiber from the Eternal City of Rome itself. The evening before the battle, Constantine sensed that this would be the final, winner-take-all fight for supremacy in the west. The opposing army was twice the size of his own and in an excellent defensive position. He knew he needed an edge – something that would inspire and motivate his troops. There are two versions of what happened next, both supposedly recounted by Constantine himself. In one, he was inspired by a divine dream, in which he saw an early Christian symbol and was promised: "by this sign, you will conquer." In a later version, the Emperor adjusted the story slightly. In the new telling, he had the vision along with his soldiers on the march after looking at the sun. In any case, the next morning, he commanded that the shields of his troops be painted with the Christian symbol, to inspire and motivate them to crush the opposition. It worked. His army defeated the army of Maxentius, and the former Emperor was drowned in the river during the fighting.

Having defeated his rival by projecting the power of the Christian faith, Constantine proceeded to demonstrate his new state of grace by fishing Maxentius's body out of the Tiber and having it decapitated. The head was stuck on a pike and paraded at the head of his army so that everyone could see what Christian mercy looked like. Later, he sent the head on tour to Carthage in North Africa to remind local authorities what they might expect if they defied him.

History doesn't record the reaction of Constantine's wife Fausta to all of this, but the defeated, headless Maxentius was actually her brother. In 307 A.D., Constantine had made a bargain with her father Maximian to marry her to forge an alliance. Clearly, family get-togethers at Constantine's house were going to continue to be a little strained.

Following his victory, Constantine followed his established pattern of erasing his rival from history – Maxentius's name and face were erased from monuments, and a systematic programme of propaganda followed to declare the former Emperor a "tyrant" and an enemy of the state while Constantine was elevated as "the liberator of the people". For good measure, any structures erected by Maxentius were re-dedicated to Constantine. Master now of the western empire, all that remained was to gain control of the east. What was needed was a unifying force, a binding element to pull it all together. Christianity was the very thing he needed.

The waves of change and shift in the religious climate between the old and new orders were certainly sensed by other sovereigns before Constantine. The simplicity of his strategy to leverage the forces of change to promote his own agenda was powerful and inspired – he would pretend to be a believer himself; he would gain the admiration of the masses by becoming one of them. If the Roman Empire had been a democracy, Constantine was going after the Christian vote.

The central principle of the Christian faith was a belief in only one God. This concept must have appealed to Constantine, who had come to believe that the Roman world should have only one Caesar and one throne, with himself on it as The Anointed Divine Representative. It was a perfect match. The old Roman belief system seemed to lack the power and strength to unite the disparate parts of the empire, so he not only accepted the usual standards but injected new blood into them, creating his own narrative out of faith, myth, and the need for celestial endorsement. He would build and shape his own storyline, and be both the director and the star of the entire production as he went.

The year after he captured Rome and dominance in the Western Empire, Constantine met with his last remaining rival – the Emperor Gaius Valerius Licianianus. Another childhood friend of Galerius, Licianianus was elevated to the senior position after Galerius had died and in 313 A.D. the last two Emperors standing decided to divide the Roman world among themselves. To seal the deal, a political marriage was arranged and Constantine's half-sister Flavia Julia Constantia became Mrs Licianianus; the occasion and celebrations generated the "Edict of Milan" proclamation, issued jointly by the two Emperors. This landmark edict officially ended all persecution of Christians across all territories in the empire, restored confiscated properties to Christian owners and congregations, and exempted Christian clergy from public civic duties. Christianity was now legal, and Constantine was in a position to shape and mould it as he wanted as its champion, advocate and defender. New churches began to be constructed all over the empire in response to the new climate, and the Emperor fostered a unique and powerful ally – the Christian church. Although not formally founded as it exists today, Constantine provided the facilities, the stage, and the authority for the church to evolve and branch out, reaching every corner of the state while building a compact base for his supremacy under the wing of the Holy Church, confirming himself as the earthly representative of the new God. It isn't difficult to imagine that both parties were delighted with the arrangement.

Over the next few years, Constantine and Licianianus ruled their respective halves of the civilised world. Constantine consolidated his power in the west, built more churches, encouraged the growth of the Christian movement and quietly assassinated anyone who looked likely to get in the way. Licianianus fought a series of wars, both internal and external, and came more and more to resent his fellow Emperor in the west, eventually sponsoring an attempt on Constantine's life. It failed. Unsatisfied, he contented himself with ordering statues of Constantine destroyed and defaced. By the year 320 A.D., Licianianus had come to appreciate and sense the great support his rival had built among the Christians. Constantine's benevolent cultivation of the blossoming religion had grown into a direct threat to his authority; the Church as a force was more loyal to Constantine than to Licianianus's Imperial system. He reacted by reneging on the Edict of Milan; the confiscation of property and dismissal of Christian office-holders began again. The final showdown arrived in 324 A.D.

The civil war that followed was brief. Constantine quickly went on the offensive, advertising that he needed to act due to his Imperial colleague's "advanced age and unpopular vices". This could loosely be translated as suggesting that Licianianus was too old and nasty a person to remain in power. It was another case of Constantine to the rescue of the downtrodden, and after a series of one-sided battles, Licianianus and his deputy Martius Martinianus finally surrendered. Constantine had publicly promised them that their lives would be spared and that they would enjoy quiet retirements as private citizens. Six months later, he accused them of plotting against the state and had them executed by hanging. Just in case, he killed Licianianus's son, too – who was also Constantine's nephew. At the end of 324 A.D. Constantine was the supreme and sole ruler of the entire Roman Empire, and to demonstrate his piety and thanks to God, he immediately renamed a city after himself. The city of Byzantium thus became Constantinople.

Now the great sponsor and champion of the Christian movement, Constantine moved to consolidate and unify the growing numbers of believers to unite in working off the same standardised script. In 325 A.D. he convened the First Council of Nicaea, a gathering of 1800 bishops and other church delegates from all over his Empire to establish standard beliefs throughout Christendom. The result was a universal playbook, settling myriad issues, such as the exact relationship between God and Jesus, the best time to celebrate Easter, and the prohibition of self-castration. It was not difficult to get universal agreement on the latter. He organised the council along the lines of the Roman senate, with himself presiding over deliberations. This was an inspired strategy, forever linking Constantine to the fortunes of the Christian church as the great and merciful patron.

Naturally, he proclaimed that delegates who didn't endorse the new rules or who supported alternative Christian belief systems should be exiled and excommunicated, declaring them "enemies of Christianity". Their doctrines, scriptures and writings were declared heretical and burned in ceremonial bonfires.

Intertwining his Imperial legacy and legitimacy with that of the church, Constantine decreed that any attempt to undermine the new "standards" for the Christian faith could bring God's divine wrath upon the Empire, threatening the very state and weakening the Emperor. Anyone who dared question the new unity of the faith could be considered under the influence of Satan, and likely to suffer eternal damnation. Questioning the rule of the Emperor now became akin to questioning God, and this was unthinkable to the believer. Constantine had assured his position and power, and as the council concluded he gave his farewell address, announcing that they had achieved unity of practice and affirming how he wanted the Church to live in harmony and peace, vowing to exemplify the best of Christian principles.

He followed up on these promised virtues the next summer by ordering the murder of his eldest son Crispus by poison and then had his wife Fausta drowned in her own bath. His reasons for doing so are still debated, but he certainly demonstrated to all his perspective heirs that he had an iron grip on the Empire and would not hesitate to eliminate his own relatives when it served his purpose. Naturally, all inscriptions and statues to their memories were amended and destroyed, as if they had never existed. Constantine was consistent in his methods, even as he portrayed himself as a paragon of virtue and the embodiment of kinder, gentler Christian values. By casting himself as the great patron of the Christians, he ensured their full support. Ever the politician, he played both sides of the field by allowing the pagans in the Empire to continue the old rituals, sacrifices and ceremonies. Christians were allowed to enjoy the illusion of greater opportunity to participate in the affairs of state and government, and many believers were to advance to high office, which was impossible before his public support. Interesting to note, however, that men from leading Roman families who declined to convert to Christianity still received appointments; at the time of his death, two-thirds of Constantine's top government officials were non-Christian pagans.

Constantine's manipulation of the new faith was masterful and complete, cementing his hold on power and changing forever the priorities of the ruling classes that came after him. The approval and endorsement of the Christian church became a necessity for legitimacy. The church would often declare the ruler as ordained and authorised by God himself; well into the 17th century, the support of the church was a requirement for the political order across Christendom. His eclectic convictions had fundamentally changed the relationship between church and state. Constantine's double game served both his own and the new clergy's ambitions equally.

Constantine's occupation moulded him to be an exceptional example of moral and religious flexibility. Only when on his deathbed did he summon a high-ranking priest to give him the absolution of the Baptismal rights. Some scholars say that it was due to a sincere belief that he could wash away all of his lifetime sins and be made penitent and pure at the end of his life. Others said he put it off as long as possible, the better to be absolved of as much sin as he could. He certainly needed this kind of deep cleansing, so his desire to prolong this ultimate dramatic moment with an actor's flair was no surprise to those close to him (or, at least, those who were left). It would be for biographers to consider if this was indeed an effort to embrace the mantle of the faithful or merely the setting up of a memorable finale by an eminent illusionist.

On his deathbed, after receiving baptism, the dying Emperor Constantine was solemnly undressed. The imperial purple robes that dignified his important position and noble descent were respectfully removed, and he was redressed in pure white linen – the simple wrappings of the novices of the faith, implying the spotless soul of the newly born. When he had breathed his last, his body was taken to his simple tomb in his church of the Apostles, led not by a procession of Roman dignitaries, but by a weeping column of priests and the faithful, with everything scripted by the Emperor in specific detail. He was laid to eternal rest among twelve Christian figures carved of marble, signifying the twelve Apostles; the last act of his Great Show was to cast himself as a Christ-figure.

As a final bow for the great pretender, it was a virtuoso performance, and Constantine deserves to take his place as one of the greatest deceivers of all time.

# THE SLEEPING DRAGON

Zhuge Liang is probably the greatest master of deception who ever lived. Known as "the Sleeping Dragon," he served as an advisor to emperor Liu Bei of the Shu Kingdom during the Three Kingdoms Period when China, as we know it now, was split between three warring groups, Shu, Wei, and Wu, each with its own claim to the seat of the Emperor. It was pretty much Game of Thrones, except that the dragons were metaphorical.

He had a meteoric rise to fame, but Zhuge Liang was not some silver spoon aristocrat who swanned into his career because of who his father was. Liang was an orphan who lived as a hermit for many years. He was a hippy, notorious for his talents at singing folk music and telling fortunes, and nothing like the tactical general he became.

Well, we all have to sell out eventually.

For Zhuge Liang, the moment came when Liu Bei showed up at the front door of his hovel, having heard of Liang's considerable powers of prediction. Any reasonable person would bend over backwards to accommodate the arrival of an emperor, but Liang slammed the door in Bei's face. It took the emperor two more visits before Liang calmly answered the door with his bags packed and a fully formed plan to conquer the whole of China.

In the battle of Bowang, his first engagement as an advisor, Liang toyed with the expectations of his opponents. In a move of astounding boldness, he sent forward his new boss and Emperor Liu Bei to challenge the opposing army personally, only to have him retreat the moment the battle had begun. Liang did this twice more, dangling the emperor as bait, to the point that his enemies were certain an ambush was coming. "But," their commander said, defying his advisors, "if their forces are so weak that they have to keep retreating then we can take any ambush they might have for us". And he was right.

The ambush came at a predictable place, and they were able to repel it quickly, although the emperor was nowhere to be seen. There was nothing left for them to do but push deeper into Liu Bei's territory. It wasn't until they had entered a narrow pass, miles down the road, still singing their victory chants, that Liang sprung his trap. In a flash, they were surrounded by a ring of fire and slaughtered one by one as they broke through the flames. Liang claimed he was able to predict their reactions to his attacks so well due to his skills at reading the I Ching: an ancient

Chinese fortune-telling method that involves reading the alignment of sticks thrown in the air.

Despite his powers of quasi-clairvoyance, Zhuge Liang still had a hard time in his new role. Liu Bei's army was vastly outnumbered by the forces of his rival emperor Cao Cao of the Wei kingdom. As much as he might sound like a sweet drink to be enjoyed on a cold day, Cao Cao was a fierce and belligerent man. He had an army of almost a million men and not a single marshmallow amongst them.

On top of this, many of Liu Bei's other advisors were jealous of the hermit Liang's grand appointment and after Zhuge Liang humiliated him in a poetry contest, a precursor to today's rap battles, the advisor Zhou Yu swore to have Liang assassinated. To do this, he set Liang the challenge of producing 100,000 arrows in 10 days - a feat that would be absolutely impossible with their resources. As it was a decree from a superior military officer, Yu was well within his rights to have Liang executed if he failed. Liang, with his typical dramatical flair, flicked his beard over his shoulder and declared he would have the arrows within three days.

Borrowing the emperor's fleet, he sailed with only a handful of men towards one of Cao Cao's castles. He ordered his men to beat the drums of war. Expecting a massive attack, the archers in the castle rained arrows down onto the ships, where Liang had cleverly placed bundles of straw in the shape of men. He had also coated the outsides of the ships in straw. When all of his vessels resembled amphibious porcupines, he ordered a retreat. The straw protected the arrows' heads, and when the full count was made at the end of the three days it was found he had stolen from their enemies almost double the requested amount of arrows!

Zhou Yu was far from happy, and not to be outdone, Yu came up with his own plan to defeat the forces of Cao Cao. At the Battle of the Red Cliffs, he too planned to send an empty fleet sailing towards Cao Cao's navy. The empty fleet would be filled with flammable materials and the few brave souls on board would crash their ships into the enemy and then set the whole thing ablaze before jumping into the water. But in the run-up to the battle, the wind was blowing in the wrong direction to spread the flames.

They say that Yu was so worried about the outcome of his plan that he began to vomit blood, but that suggests he probably had some serious pre-existing health issues. Liang spent four days straight praying for the winds to change, and when they finally did, Yu thanked him by sending his two best assassins after him. Liang was expecting this and was able to lie low until the battle had been won and Yu was too busy being praised to come after him again.

It is speculated that Yu's plan only worked because of Cao Cao's idiocy. Cao Cao had far greater numbers of troops, but they weren't experienced, sailors. He crammed them onto ships to speed their advance, but ultimately it left them vulnerable. After years of bitter rivalry, and having never overcome Liang, Zhou Yu succumbed to his health problems.

He died cursing the fact that he had to be born in the same world as the great Zhuge Liang.

Zhuge Liang's powers were indeed great, but even his brilliant mind couldn't find a way to cheat death. His master and Emperor Liu Bei died before his dream of uniting China was accomplished. His final wish was that Liang raise his son to be a great ruler, and if that wasn't possible, Liang was to rule in his son's place. Liu Bei's son was a worthy successor to his father, but his youth was a worry to many of his supporters. No one wants to be ordered around by a kid. And so, the kingdom of Shu began to fracture. Smaller groups lead by local warlords declared their independence. It became like Mad Max but with horses instead of cars. So Liang had to travel south to resolve these conflicts.

In one battle, he fought the great bandit warlord Men Huo. Men Huo was a proud man, and rightly so, for he was a virtuoso in the art of skull-crushing. But a battle against Zhuge Liang is not as simple as popping a head like a watermelon. He was outmanoeuvred at every turn and found himself captured. Tied up and brought before Liang he claimed that it was not a real fight as he didn't get the opportunity to crush any skulls. Zhuge Liang set him free and said he would try and be fairer the next time, but it wasn't long before Men Huo was tied up again. Still, Huo raged that the terms were not reasonable, that Liang's soldiers should stay in the open and allow their skulls to be crushed, but Liang was never one to surrender a tactical advantage. He told the warlord as much and sent him on his way again. This happened a total of seven times before Men Huo finally surrendered to Liang's strength, acknowledging that there was more than one way to be strong. He joined the forces of Shu.

It was during this campaign that Zhuge Liang tried his luck at deceiving even the gods themselves. When his army came to a raging torrent on a flooded river that they needed to cross, the locals told him that their river god was angry and that only an offering of human heads would suffice. Liang's soldiers advised him to find more bandits and offer their heads, but Liang was too noble for the sacrifice even of his enemies. Besides, as with Men Huo, he knew the barbarians were more useful as allies. And so, he came up with a delicious solution. He created a pork dumpling to resemble a human head. They are known as Mantou or "Barbarian Head Dumplings" and still enjoyed to this day. Liang threw hundreds of them into the river, and soon the surface was calm enough for safe passage. Apparently, the gods are idiots. Or, those are some amazing dumplings.

Of course, this story is probably apocryphal, as was that of his turning the direction of the wind through prayer. There is also a story of how Zhuge Liang turned back an invading army by constructing a maze of stones on the ground that was inspired by his divinations – though that story comes into a different light when we consider that Liang is credited with the invention of the landmine. But the fact that a mystical explanation of events endures to this day is telling. What better way could a benevolent trickster make sure that his well-meaning ideas carried on into the future than to make himself a legend?

Picture a smart man in a superstitious age. Of course, he would use that superstition to his advantage. There are arguments that all forms of fortune-telling stem from cold reading: the skill of letting your audience feed you information when you give them open-ended cues to interpret.

It's the same when a TV psychic says. "I feel a presence. It feels like a female presence. An… an old woman?" "My Aunt Caroline," shouts an audience member, and the ruse grows from there.

This kind of divination has emerged in cultures all across the globe, aided by the fact that before the rise of widely accessible literature, people would have vivid hallucinations all the time. It was a form of proto-therapy, allowing people to process emotions about lost loved ones and fears about their future. Opening these emotions to another, especially a stranger who claims to have supernatural powers, can leave a person vulnerable. A smart man could exploit that vulnerability for his own personal gain. As many still do today, he could rise to great power and riches using these skills. In a more superstitious time, and with shrewd management of his fame, he could make himself a legend. Perhaps that was Zhuge Liang's greatest deception of all.

But Zhuge Liang did finally meet his match. Perhaps not quite his intellectual equal, but with far greater resources and none of Cao Cao's idiocy. Liang was defeated by the Wei general, Siam Yi. They fought the longest and bloodiest campaign of the entire Three Kingdoms war. Both sides were forced to retreat in turn, both suffered huge losses, even though

Liang was trying to minimise the loss of life on his side while Siam Yi employed his greater numbers recklessly and to significant effect.

Eventually, the stress of it all killed Liang. But that was not before Liang had his last laugh.

After a series of defeats, Yi had made Liang desperate. His army was walled up in a small village with Yi's forces fast approaching. Liang had lost too many good men already on this campaign and was determined to lose no more.

He was too smart to go down fighting a battle he knew he couldn't win. Instead, he sent the majority of his army away. They could ride back into Shu lands and be safe, but he needed to buy them some time. To do this, he requested that a hundred of his best men stay behind. He sent them around the village to find the least convincing disguises they could, and when they were all dressed up, he left the gates of the village-wide open.

When Sima Yi reached the village, he found Liang sitting on the walls above the open gate. Liang was playing his lute, the picture of the serene folk-singing hermit he had once been. Liang's reputation as a strategic mastermind was such that Yi was sure this was a trap. There was no way Liang could have left himself this vulnerable. And so, Yi ordered his army to retreat. By the time he realised he had been tricked, Zhuge Liang had taken his entire army safely home, without a single drop of blood being spilt.

# INDULGENCES

A brief disclaimer to start this chapter: this is not an attack on the present-day Catholic Church. It will be talking about the medieval era, a time when the people of Europe believed that there were witches, that the planet was flat, and that their kings were directly chosen by God.

Most people in this world were illiterate, and the lucky ones died at 30. This is not a debate about the validity of organised religion or the existence of God. This is the story of how the Bible was deliberately mistranslated to make a few people extremely rich, renovate a couple of cathedrals, and fund a handful of holy wars.

This is the story of one of the greatest and most widespread cons of all time. This is the story of Indulgences.

It should be common knowledge that Christianity is based on the idea that people who do good things (saving drowning puppies, helping old ladies to cross the street, killing non-believers) go to heaven, a place where good things (all you can eat pizza, backgammon tournaments, smiles from cute angels) happen to you eternally. People who do bad things on the other hand (drowning puppies, pushing old ladies into the street, doubting the awesomeness of God) go to hell, a place where – I'm sure you can see where this is going.

But around the 12th Century, an important question was raised: what happens if you aren't really good or bad? Is it a tipping scale where St Peter agonisingly balances the puppies you drowned on one side and the puppies you saved on the other and whichever way it tipped points to the door for you?

No, the Catholic God is forgiving, and so there is always a chance for redemption. The papal decree was that no one goes to hell on a technicality. Those that have sinned (read: everyone) but have confessed their sins (read: Catholics) go to Purgatory when they die. Purgatory is a place that should be familiar to you if you stuck it out with the TV show "Lost," up until its whimpering finale, or have ever been to the waiting area of a bus station, motor vehicles office or any doctor's office. You could look at it as being friend-zoned by God. There is the promise of heaven in the future, but you have to wait until you are accepted, perhaps indefinitely.

# INDULGENCES

Like the friend zone, the existence of Purgatory is the subject of much debate, but for Catholics, in the medieval period, it was a certainty. Everyone sinned, everyone confessed, and everyone worked up a little post-death waiting time before they could waltz on through the pearly gates.

Because of this, a sort of points-based system emerged in the Catholic community. All sins short of murder had an associated waiting time that would be tallied up as you confessed to them. People had a pretty accurate reckoning of how long they would have to spend waiting once they took their dirt nap before they could get to the backgammon, the cute angels, and the pizza buffet. They were also told of a whole slew of pious actions – frequently, vast numbers of Hail Marys or other forms of genuflection - that would reduce that time. If you felt you had too much free time, you could even pray on behalf of dead relatives. But all of this praying did take up a lot of time and could be considered quite tedious. Why waste time that could be spent having fun (and probably adding to your time in Purgatory)?

Just like the terrifying mobile games with their clashing clans and their castles developers today take a week of real-world time to build, the Church agreed that all of that waiting time was a terrible thing, and offered to make it all go away – for a reasonable fee.

This was the birth of Indulgences.

By making a charitable donation to the Church, your time in purgatory could be made to vanish. It was as simple as that. As one medieval rhyme put it, "As soon as the coin in the coffer rings, the soul from purgatory springs".

I'm sure it was catchier in the original German.

In a coincidence that should be shocking to no one in our modern world of applied scarcity capitalism, around the time that Indulgences became widespread, other forms of absolution became almost useless. It wasn't long before the amount of time you needed to pray while living to avoid time in purgatory was longer than your life itself. It's a wonder they didn't start charging extra for access to a deluxe version of heaven with a cocktail bar at the buffet and where the cute angels would sit on your lap.

It's unclear precisely who first came up with the idea of an Indulgence (possibly because they became wealthy enough to have that part of history rewritten), but it is hard to blame just one person when they were being signed by bishops and archbishops all across Europe for over three hundred years. Some even bear the signature of the Pope himself. But one of the most infamous dispensers of Indulgences was the bishop Johann Tetzel.

Tetzel was the Grand Commissioner of Indulgences in Germany. He took so much money under the guise of saving souls that in his most famous remaining portrait he is swearing an oath not on a bible but on a coin box. His sermons frequently dealt with the idea of Purgatory and were, in effect, one long sales pitch on buying Indulgences to avoid an afterlife of numbing neutrality. When he ran out of living believers who could pay their way out of purgatory, he started selling indulgences for their dead relatives! Even though you might think that would be a well that would never run dry, he took it a step further than that and started selling people Indulgences for future sins that they had yet to commit. No matter how devout you were, Tetzel could find a way to sell you an Indulgence.

His hard graft paid off, too: Tetzel is credited with funding huge refurbishments to St. Peter's Basilica, one of the most, if not the most, impressive buildings ever constructed by the Catholic Church. And that wasn't even half of what he took because a big chunk of the money went to pay off the vast debts that his boss, Albert of Brandenburg, amassed in rising to the rank of cardinal. Why he had to pay off his boss's debts is unclear, but we can assume he probably didn't have much choice in the matter. This was, after all, the age of the Inquisition.

The Inquisition was the Catholic secret police force, busting down people's doors at night - similar to the KGB, except they came around to check whether you believed that a man in a big hat spoke the word of God verbatim. The Inquisition had so much influence that it was above the local law, rounding people up and torturing them until they confessed to whatever it was that the Inquisition wanted them to confess to. This, of course, was done to save the souls of their victims. They burned thousands of women at the stake under suspicions of witchcraft (read: campaigning for equal rights), and stamped out many smaller Christian sects, branding them as heretics. To add an extra level of terror to Tetzel's character, he had previously worked as the Grand Inquisitor in Poland.

There is a famous story about Tetzel, spread by Martin Luther (more on him later): One night travelling through Leipzig, Tetzel was paid an enormous sum by a noble seeking an Indulgence to pardon a future sin. Presumably rubbing his hands together with glee, Tetzel agreed. However, on the road out of Leipzig, Tetzel was set upon by a masked bandit. After savagely beating Tetzel and relieving him of his money, the bandit removed his mask, revealing himself to be none other than that same nobleman!

He thanked Tetzel for his advance pardon and went on his way, guilt-free.

It's a charming story of just desserts, but when you consider that Tetzel was the former commander of the Catholic torture-police, it seems a lot less likely.

Tetzel was far from the only one selling Indulgences. They were such big business that it was hard to keep it within the upper echelons of the Church or even within the Church at all. People made a living as professional "Pardoners", going around calculating how much you would owe for your various sins and writing you up a personalised Indulgence then and there. In another not-so-shocking twist, it turned out that many of these Pardoners weren't priests at all and that they were effectively selling ludicrously expensive signatures.

I'll avoid making the obvious joke here about that not being too different from what the church was selling for fear of pulling at a thread that will leave all of humanity as nothing more than monkeys in silly hats. But yes, Indulgences were big business. They had to be. It was a period of rapid expansion for the Catholic Church. They were sanctioning holy wars all over the place. They reclaimed Spain and Portugal from Islamic rule over a period of 500 hundred years and for good measure continued their expansion into northern Africa and the Middle East until they had reclaimed the majority of the early Christian world. They called these wars the Crusades.

Because they were holy wars, it was the obligation of all good Christians to fight for their God. If you didn't have a good excuse not to fight (there weren't many) you would have to answer to the Inquisition. But if you did happen to be too old, infirm, or wealthy to fight, you could always support the troops with an Indulgence instead. Once they had significantly redesigned the maps of their age, the Catholic Church then set their sights on a new destination: Latin America, a continent that is still predominantly Catholic today.

It's unclear exactly when the practice of selling Indulgences was stopped, but it probably had something to do with the Reformation. The Reformation was the most significant schism the Christian faith has ever seen, and like all great moments in Christianity, it all started with something being nailed to a piece of wood.

The something was Martin Luther's Ninety-five Theses, a scathing document about making Christianity more accessible to the common people, calling out Tetzel by name for charging people for salvation, and arguably claiming that the poor couldn't afford to get into heaven. This was the protest that started Protestantism.

Luther translated the Bible into common vernacular, getting away from the Latin that the average person couldn't understand. As an example of how little the average church-goer understood of what they heard: the magical phrase "hocus pocus" is actually a mishearing of the phrase "hoc es mea corpus", meaning "this is my body" from the communion rites.

It's probable that once believers could actually understand their holy book, they came to realise that there wasn't anything that directly mentioned Purgatory, let alone Indulgences. We can also assume that priests were a bit more careful about scamming their congregation with the hip new competition down the street.

But, you may be asking, why wasn't Protestantism stamped out by the Inquisition? That's how the Church dealt with all its previous opponents. The thing was, all those former "heretics" didn't have the backing of a monarch. Protestantism, however, happened to come along just when Henry VIII of England was having an argument with the pope over whether or not he was married to Catherine of Aragon.

They couldn't agree, and so the Reformation found itself with a mighty powerful ally. It wasn't long after that the Catholic Church issued an official decree condemning the abuse of Indulgences. They do still exist in a profoundly altered form today, one much closer to a charitable donation to the Church.

There is also still a belief in purgatory but the penance required to negate your time there is a lot more manageable, capable of being done in an afternoon rather than a lifetime. Now, we can be thankful that there is no one religion in our society with so much power that they think they can get away with a scam such as Indulgences, but there are plenty of individuals like Tetzel seeking to exploit people's faith for their own personal gain.

Perhaps the lesson to be gained from this is: don't spend money on something that you can't see, but thinking like that might be the end of the modern finance industry.

# POYAIS

$A$ swashbuckling dandy with a taste for excess and high fashion is

possibly not a person naturally associated with a major property swindle

but, then again, Donald Trump is not a persona inherently coupled with the

Presidency of the US, yet there he is – for all to see! A Scottish war veteran

descended from the infamous Rob Roy, Gregor MacGregor was born in

the picturesque Loch Katrine in the Scottish Highlands region of

Trossachs, 30 km north of Glasgow. Ironically, the name 'Katrine' comes

from the Gaelic, meaning Highland Robber – a title usually bestowed on

Rob Roy but equally apt for his less famous descendant Gregor

MacGregor. Although Gregor managed to pull off one of the greatest acts

of fraud in history, his name is rarely acknowledged. Even those seeking the

famous man in the Loch Katrine cemetery will find no trace of this

dangerous narcissist who raised the equivalent of millions of pounds and

convinced hundreds of impassioned settlers to set sail to the unknown land

of Poyais.

MacGregor's claim to fame is that he pulled off one of the biggest, longest-running and most financially rewarding scams in history. Accumulating somewhere in the region of £3.6 billion in today's money, MacGregor didn't just sell a plot or a house or even an estate – he sold a whole country. And it didn't exist! Poyais was the product of MacGregor's imagination. It had the clearest, cleanest streams; plentiful fish and wild game; fertile soils capable of producing three wheat crops a year; friendly natives, ample gold and a thriving seaside town.

Not a robber *per se*, but nevertheless able to extract money from people with apparent ease, MacGregor followed in Rob Roy MacGregor's footsteps as part extortionist and part hero. Gregor MacGregor was a war veteran with a strong reputation, having captured Amelia Island in 1817 after a month of tumultuous fighting. However, his war efforts were not all glorious, and two years later he abandoned his troops in New Granada, returning to Scotland in 1821 with some big words and even bigger claims. MacGregor's super scam began with the news that he had been bestowed with the undoubted honour of being made the Cazique or Prince of a little-known colony named Poyais. It appears that King George Frederic Augustus, the ostensible leader of the Mosquito Coast, had decided, within his somewhat titular powers, to bestow this blessing onto MacGregor. In recognition of what? No-one really knows. King George was a king in inherited name and title, but wielded little power, bowing to the superior authority of the British Crown. Still, no one in Scotland was to suspect this, so MacGregor's claim was just as believable as the concept that spaghetti grows on trees – something the BBC managed to convince hundreds of viewers of on April Fool's Day in 1957.

Some of the biggest lies, it seems, are the ones that are easiest to believe. Some would have us believe the first landing on the moon was an enormous hoax (and maybe it was). Hitler convinced vast swathes of the German population that the Jews were solely and completely responsible for their loss in the First World War. In these days of all-encompassing cyberspace, it's possible to find evidence to support almost any lie, and, conversely, to disprove almost any alleged truth. For those like MacGregor, Ponzi or Madoff, it is not the lie that counts, or even the gravity of the falsehood – it's about finding your niche audience and creating a story that will consume them, absorb them, engage them and make them believe that no other option is even remotely as tempting as the one you have to offer.

For MacGregor, proper timing was everything, and he was fortunate enough to exist during a financial climate that lent itself to blind and blasé investments. After Napoleon's defeat, the economy of the United Kingdom was enjoying steady expansion, with manufacturing as its driving force. Workers within the industrial sector were, at last, enjoying a period of relative abundance, with wages increasing as the cost of living started to fall. While the British had traditionally invested in their own government's bonds, the returns were low and, although the investment was secure, it also lacked the excitement that accompanies the promise of a quick buck. Consequently, investors sought a greater thrill and higher returns by indulging in what financial journalist David Evans described as "sanguine anticipations of inordinate gain." Translated into layman's English, that would mean optimistic expectations of disproportionate returns.

It was into this expectant economic boom that MacGregor sailed on his return from battling away in Venezuela, and he must have believed he had already landed in his own personal Never-Never Land! People were desperate for new financial opportunities and memories of their failed attempts at colonisation made the concept of a ready-made heaven on earth for the Scottish even more appealing. Playing to his audience, MacGregor rode the investment wave while financiers happily threw good money after bad. In October 1822, MacGregor was ready to go live and, in keeping with rates paid by various Latin American governments, offered a Poyais bond of £200,000 at 6%. To ease any doubt in potential investors' minds, MacGregor argued that this lush and abundant paradise enjoyed plentiful natural resources which meant the export taxes would generate enough revenue to comfortably cover interest payments on the debt.

Fundamentally, like shady estate agents all over the world, MacGregor sold a dream and that dream was invented and cultivated to suit the expectations and aspirations of his fellow countrymen. Not only would they be embarking on one of the greatest treasure hunts of all time, but they would also have the opportunity to prove the bravery of Scottish stock by creating their first colony. Envious of the vast swathes of land that neighbours England had secured for themselves, the Scots' own attempts had been well and truly scuppered, largely and consistently by the English! In 1698, the Darien scheme, aimed at colonising either side of the Panama isthmus effectively given Scotland great powers, was stymied by the English. The scheme had the potential, both in terms of circumventing a dangerous voyage across America and in securing what could have been a precursor to the Panama Canal, to make Scotland a truly international power.

This was a key piece of history for MacGregor, who believed not only that he was descended from an Inca princess, but also that he was avenging the downfall of one of his ancestors who had played a part in the Darien catastrophe. At this time, while his Poyais was just beginning, MacGregor is thought to have had genuine intentions about the colonisation of this remote land – he knew Central America well and had fought there for both the British and Venezuelan armies – he had an insider knowledge that gave him both authority and power. The fact that he had no real rights to the land would have been almost insignificant to a man of his arrogance. In his book The Land That Never Was, (2004) David Sinclair places heavy emphasis on how MacGregor's military career taught him how to create the illusion of prosperity and victory in the face of defeat, teaching him the art of fabrication and self-belief.

Comparable to the dot-com madness of the 1980s, the mania that gripped Scotland during the early 19th century lead to a craze of conjecture surrounding the abundant wealth awaiting the brave Highlanders willing to cross the seas and start anew. With immigration to the Americas as popular as throwing money at bonds, this was the perfect time for MacGregor to float his fantastical boat. The maps and statistics he professionally presented in a leather-bound guidebook and the supporting manuscript by the mysterious Thomas Strangeways (who turned out to be none other than Gregor MacGregor himself), made the evidence clear – the climate was good, the natives friendly and soil fertile. Rivers ran with clear, sparkling water, under which could be found plentiful reserves of gold. Poyais was close enough to the Isthmus of Panama, where plans were already in the offing for a monumental canal that would facilitate trading worldwide that it promised great wealth both immediately and in the long run.

This was the fantasy that MacGregor offered, but it is not only the story but how the narrative unfolds that bears witness to his capacity for both self-promotion and self-aggrandisement. As he embellished his military exploits, the British press caught on and presented him as a cavalier champion. His dubious past was swept under a regal carpet woven from his association with the Die-Hards, as the 57th Regiment of Foot had become known. Having served with this division as a teenager, MacGregor managed to retain it as something of a feather in his cap, despite his other military debacles. With international news being intermittent at best and downright inaccurate at worst, MacGregor managed to emerge smelling of roses. As the countries and governments throughout Latin America were constantly changing hands and power shifted in a perpetual state of flux, MacGregor's claims did not seem wildly unbelievable.

On his return to London, members of its more sophisticated society embraced the exotic-looking Cazique and rumours of his sovereignty flourished. The arrival of his enigmatic second wife, Josefa MacGregor, assisted in fuelling the fire. With MacGregor's penchant for elaborate insignia and his obsession with personal appearance, he managed to infiltrate the higher echelons of influential London society, while his sterner critics depicted him as a disreputable character who loved parties as much as he purported to love Poyers (his name for the indigenous inhabitants of Poyais). Fun, but dangerous, MacGregor started putting into place some serious building blocks for his new nation, devising a complex tricameral government. This three-tiered parliament is an uncommon concept but was used by South Africa during Apartheid to co-opt Coloureds and Indians while maintaining a separation of power that worked entirely in favour of the white minority. Clearly, MacGregor had the acumen to back up his lies and, while he created elaborate constitutional agreements for his country, he simultaneously charmed, advertised, coerced and even found the time to design intricate uniforms for the fabricated regiments of his non-existent Poyaisian Army.

A crowning stroke in MacGregor's campaign was gaining the alliance and support of Major William John Richardson who subsequently created a British base for the Poyaisian royals at his estate of Oak Hall in Wanstead. With all the pomp and circumstance a man of his standing could have dreamt of, MacGregor appointed him as the top representative of his Never Never Land, going so far as to present a letter of credence to George IV, which MacGregor signed with great audacity as "Gregor the First, Sovereign Prince of the State of Poyais.

With all this embellishment, it's tempting to believe MacGregor's story over 200 years later. Why create a government for a land that doesn't exist? Why design uniforms that would never be worn? In truth, it seems MacGregor was living a dream and in living it, almost began to believe it himself – leaving the whole story hovering on a fence between fraud and fantasy. This type of grandiose behaviour is symptomatic of a narcissistic personality type which his obsession with his own magnificence also attests to. With his grand titles and what his contemporary, Colonel Michael Rafter, describes as "an extreme affectation of dress and fashion," MacGregor shows certain indications of narcissistic tendencies. In common with other famous narcissists, such as Adolf Hitler, MacGregor was preoccupied with power and prestige and happy to manipulate others who he perceived as lesser beings to his greatly superior self. A dreamer by nature, MacGregor's belief that he was descended from an Inca princess suggests he believed his role of patrician of a new country his fundamental birthright.

Along with the ability to manipulate others and reinvent himself, MacGregor was a natural conman with an intuition that enabled him to identify his victims and speak to them using tactics that would intensify the magnetism of his offer. According to Maria Konnikova, MacGregor artfully combined two forms of persuasion that appeal to different facets of human behaviour. When convincing a person to commit to something, there needs to be both push and pull; the push is the drive that encourages them to act, while the pull is removing the torpor that prevents them from taking the first step. Tory Higgins, a psychologist at Columbia University, asserts that while some of us are more inclined to be attracted by the potential positives of the outcome, others are focussed on the negatives and seek out options that will limit loss. In his sales pitch, MacGregor managed the perfect juxtaposition between the pull and the push.

Appealing to the courage and audacity that Scottish Highlanders prided themselves on, MacGregor made investing in Poyais seem like both a gift and a challenge at the same time: it would only be the bravest, cleverest men who would earn a place in his great kingdom. Simultaneously, he referred interested parties to the prospectus written by Dr Strangeways, giving his claims third-party authority, albeit that the third party in question was actually himself. In asking people to invest a small amount (the equivalent of the average working man's daily income), he was selling them a dream for a few shillings - common-or-garden folk could buy a piece of paradise and the opportunity of a lifetime. The final nail in the coffin was that this amazing chance of a new life was going to slip through Scottish fingers if they didn't act fast. If the Scots didn't populate Poyais, then someone, probably rival Englishmen, would snap it up in no time. MacGregor gave interviews to newspapers and wined and dined influential socialites while creating a convoluted honours system for his new republic. What was not to believe?

MacGregor was so convincing that not only did he secure investment, he also managed to convince hundreds of people, primarily Scotsmen like himself, to sign up to emigrate. Once seven ships were filled, the first two set sail, containing doctors, tradesman and other people of high standing. With willing settlers ready for the off, the notion of investing in his grand scheme became even more attractive. Potential financiers were clearly under the impression that it wasn't possible that these intelligent individuals would embark on a dangerous sea voyage unless there was something concrete at the end of it. Furthermore, their imminent arrival in Poyais meant that financial returns would be materialising any day. And so, his story developed its own momentum and tumbled off to the horizon in a flap of sails and the creak of a wooden deck.

The Honduras Packet and its 70 naïve passengers set sail under the leadership of ex-British Army officer, Hector Hall. They would be the first to set foot on the 8,000,000 acres Cazique MacGregor ruled. Once reaching dry land, they expected to see sparkling rivers of clear water; vast tracts of fertile land ready for sowing; fish leaping in the waters while wild (but gentle) animals gambolled through the hills and a blossoming town with mansions, paved streets, a theatre, cathedral and even the infamous Bank of Poyais. On 10 September 1822, MacGregor met with the pioneers, offering them the best of luck and issuing newly printed Bank of Poyais dollar notes. Suddenly, for these ambitious, courageous people, the dream had become a reality. Biographer David Sinclair asserts, "The people … who had planned to take their savings with them in coin, were also delighted to exchange their gold for the legal currency of Poyais." Thus, the scam enters its final death throes.

Less than six months later, the second consignment of unsuspecting con victims took to the seas in the Kennersley Castle, departing from Leith on 22 January 1823. In what was perceived to be a gesture of great generosity, MacGregor went aboard and announced that, as this was a maiden voyage from the homelands of Scotland to the new horizons of Poyais, all women and children would travel free of charge. As he was rowed back to shore, MacGregor's ears were ringing with the cheers emanating from his future settlers.

While the Honduras Packet was still on its way to a much-anticipated destination, back in Scotland finances were starting to look a little shaky for MacGregor. In an attempt to separate himself from the republican movement in Latin America, Gregor was desperately trying to ingratiate himself with the Spanish, who brushed him off like an annoying fly. As political instability threatened South America, so the desire to invest in this other world declined and, in its place, came a flurry of selling. MacGregor's cash flow dried up, and Poyaisian investments slumped. Meanwhile, the settlers arrived at their promised land in November 1822 only to gaze at a desolate shore with looks of confusion and perturbation.

As they contemplated the wasteland before them, searching for signs of the famous St Joseph Cathedral, so the folks on board the Honduras Packet simply and trustingly assumed that they had, by some navigational error, arrived in the wrong place. Gregor's nominated leader, Hector Hall, was less sure but nonetheless oversaw as they set up a makeshift camp on the oceanfront. After numerous search parties returned with little to report and the Poyaisian authorities failed to pitch up and welcome their new inhabitants, so Hall began to put a little more faith into his hunch – they'd been duped! But, for fear of the chaos that would ensue among the emigrants should he air his suspicions, Hall kept quiet, reassuring them that it was only a matter of time before they were found and taken to the land of milk and honey. After several weeks, Hall took it upon himself to sail off into a fierce storm, announcing on his departure that he was heading out to Cape Gracias a Dios in the hopes of finding the Mosquito king. The pioneers sat abandoned on a beach with only their dreams and a few months of provisions to live on.

Who were these people? Who were the gullible chumps who'd thrown their lives away on the strength of a man's word and a dubious piece of paper? According to Boston University's Tamar Frankel, the victims of financial scams have tended throughout history to follow a certain pattern. MacGregor had focussed his attention on people he felt had a natural affinity with him. The people he targeted as investors were not the same as those he sought as his new Poyais citizens. The Scots men and women he looked to for this role fell into two general types, according to Frankel. The one group demonstrated a willingness to believe; a higher than average tolerance for risk, and the need, much like MacGregor, to be part of an elite group, believing themselves to better or more educated than the general hoi polloi. The similarities between this group and MacGregor are self-evident. The second faction exhibits dissatisfaction and often begrudges others who have a higher economic status, leading to a readiness to take precarious risks to improve their lot.

MacGregor's desire to connect with those who felt a kinship with him is a trait of all so-called "affinity fraud", defined by the Association of Certified Fraud Examiners as "a financial scheme practice that relies on building trust with victims based on shared affiliations and characteristics … for financial gain." MacGregor was one of them, he came from the same stock, he shared their ethnic group – for many, it was incomprehensible that he might have betrayed them! Even after several months on the barren island that was supposed to be Poyais, most of the country's new settlers still believed in MacGregor, firmly regarding the whole incident as either a misunderstand or the result of another's incompetence or untruth.

These trusting emigrants were still on the beach, anxiously awaiting their dream future, when the rainy seasons blew in, bringing insects and disease with them. The fair-skinned Scots and their associates had little defence against malaria or yellow fever, and soon a sense of despair was tangible. Poor leadership had led to squabbles over rations and expeditions to hunt and gather food lacked direction. As the weather worsened and disease started to take the lives of the younger and weaker among them, so the émigrés sank further into despondency. Finally, in May 1923, five months after their buoyant departure from Great Britain, the remaining settlers were discovered by a schooner, the Mexican Eagle, as it transported the Chief Magistrate of Belize to the Mosquito king's court. Although offered safe passage to British Honduras, most of the group decided to stay where they were, awaiting the return of their leader, Hector Hall. A few days later, Hall arrived with the Mosquito king himself in tow, but this wasn't to be the salvation the beach dwellers had imagined. Rather than granting them a spectacular paradise on which to make their fortunes, the king revoked MacGregor's land claim and declared that the Cazique had never been granted such a title nor given the right to sell land or use it to raise funds. The king continued to explain that, as they were on his land, they had the choice of leaving or pledging allegiance to him, the rightful lord of the land. What choice did they have? They took their meagre possessions and left, leaving behind the dead and those too sick to survive the journey to Belize.

Even as they arrived in the comparative safety of Belize, there was little respite. The overcrowding on the schooner had taken its toll on the settlers, and the weather had worsened further, causing disease to spread even more rapidly. Approximately 250 people left Great Britain for the promised land of Poyais but only 50 ever returned. The death toll would have have been much higher were it not for Major-General Edward Codd, his Majesty's Superintendent and Commander-in-chief at Belize, Honduras who proceeded to open an enquiry into how the imaginary land of Poyais had come into existence, subsequently sending word back to London of the suffering of the original settlers. As a result, the five ships that had already left for Poyais were intercepted by the Royal Navy and sent back to their country of origin, saving hundreds of lives.

With the typical lack of consideration associated with narcissists, MacGregor exhibited little remorse, leaving London before the survivors landed on 12 October 1823. Possibly because of Codd's investigation, the London press was full of news of Poyais and the associated scandal, publicly accusing MacGregor of an enormous fraud that had cost innocent people their lives. But the survivors remained true to their Cazique and claimed the newspapers were misrepresenting them, going so far as to sign an affidavit declaring, "[W]e believe that Sir Gregor MacGregor has been worse used by Colonel Hall and his other agents than was ever a man before... and had they done their duty by Sir Gregor and by us, things would have turned out very differently at Poyais".

While others protested on his behalf, MacGregor issued statements indicating that he had been the victim of embezzlement and that Poyais still existed, ready and waiting for development, were it not for the jealous critters in British Honduras trying to undo his great deeds. Even as his dream had turned into a nightmare, taking the lives of children and trusting countrymen, MacGregor held on tight, moving his claims and sales pitch across the English Channel to France. He continued trying to woo the Spanish, with little success but much hubris, even writing to the King of Spain at the end of 1824 proclaiming himself a "descendant of the ancient Kings of Scotland". While the Spanish found his advances of little importance or significance, MacGregor found a warmer reception in Paris and succeeded in convincing Gustavus Butler Hippisley, a comrade in arms from his military days in Latin America, of Poyais' existence and promising future. Hippisley was employed by MacGregor in March 1825 and helped him negotiate a deal to sell over 60% of his imaginary land to a French company for their own settlement.

Maybe, by this time, MacGregor was experiencing something akin to responsibility for the deaths he had inadvertently caused and was, as biographer Sinclair suggests, trying to distance himself from any further disasters occurring on arrival at the non-existent settlement. Then again, maybe not. MacGregor continued to pursue new investments into his falsified country and, in August 1825, published a new constitution for Poyais, changing it from a kingdom to a republic but retaining for himself the title of Cazique in recognition of his new role as head of State. The French company, owned by Lehuby, prepared the ship to make the first trip to Poyais with the first French settlers. These unsuspecting travellers applied for passports to travel to Poyais, causing suspicion amongst government officials which resulted in the ship being kept in port pending a resolution of their suspicions. Meanwhile, the would-be settlers became distinctly unsettled and reported their concerns to the police, leading to arrest of two of MacGregor's staff, including Hippisley.

Lehuby and MacGregor fled, although MacGregor was found and arrested three months later and faced charges alongside Hippisley and his former secretary, Irving. MacGregor remained incredulous, suggesting that a sudden change in law had been brought about by jealous Frenchmen – or possibly even the scandalous Spanish – to challenge Poyais as it sought its independence under the benevolent Cazique's leadership. A bare-faced lie, perhaps, but maybe MacGregor believed it – throughout this sorry scam, there does seem to be an underlying thread of self-delusion. In a statement he issued from prison, MacGregor claimed he was "held, prisoner… for reasons of which he is not aware" and was being punished for his attempts at being one of the "founders of independence in the New World." Self-deluded or not, MacGregor managed to convince the courts of his innocence and, in the end, only Lehuby, the owner of the French company duped into buying up over half of Poyais, was found guilty of the charges laid against him.

None of this appears to have fazed MacGregor and he immediately hot-footed it back to London where he proceeded to sell a slightly less elaborate version of the same scam, with himself now acting as just the Cacique of the Republic of Poyais. Although this third attempt was less successful, it seems its downfall was more to do with the lack of profits generated by the previous investments rather than of any suspicion that Poyais didn't actually exist. Sinclair asserts that "Some investors had begun to understand that they were being fleeced, but almost none realised how comprehensively." In fact, between England and Scotland, MacGregor continued to reinvent his scam repeatedly over the next nine years, until finally abandoning it in 1838. Having spanned 17 years, it must be one of the longest-running fraud schemes in history and truly was MacGregor's life's work.

MacGregor's ability to continually redesign the same scam and successfully sell it more than once is a testament to his brilliance. Modern-day comparisons don't come close to the longevity of MacGregor's scheme.

In the UK earlier this year, a couple was arrested for an extensive property fraud scam that had spanned six years and involved victims the length and breadth of Britain. The criminals earned a sum total of £1.7 million – a drop in the ocean given that MacGregor managed to amount the equivalent (in today's economy) of £3.6 billion during his lengthy crime.

And good old MacGregor got away with it! Just a few nights in prison and then a life of Reilly. After his second wife's death in 1838, MacGregor returned to Venezuela where he was welcomed with open arms as a veteran hero of the War of Independence. He subsequently settled there as a citizen and received a pension in recognition of his service and, when he died, aged 59, he was buried with full military honours in Caracas Cathedral. Poyais didn't fare so well and remains an undeveloped wasteland even today.

It is worth considering whether MacGregor would have been quite so successful in the modern world. With international news, fraud alerts and improved methods of detection, it's possible that his Poyais scheme would have fallen on deaf ears. The current financial climate also lends itself to caution rather than "sanguine anticipations of inordinate gain." Maybe if he had hit the dot.com mania, he would have found his niche selling cyberspace to eager speculators – certainly, the sophistication of con-artistry could have given many a run for their money, quite literally. A star performer with the intelligence to back up his claims, MacGregor surpasses other fraudsters with similar intentions throughout history. Perhaps it was the sheer magnitude of his plan that made it so convincing. Alternatively, MacGregor might have sought out modern-day Utah where more affinity crimes are committed than anywhere else in the world. Is this because the people of Utah are gullible or stupid? Possibly neither. Church-based affinity crimes are the most common simply because there is a group of people who have complete faith in a trusted leader. The con-man draws in the leader, and the rest of the flock will follow until they are all suitably fleeced.

No doubt, if MacGregor had lived today, he would have headed straight for Utah. With 60% of the population being Mormon whose friendly openness exposes their unsuspecting jugular to any opportunistic scammer, MacGregor could probably have sold them America with his capacity for lies and self-aggrandisement. As Senator Ben McAdams asserts about Utahns, "… one of our greatest strengths, which is we see the best in others, and we're entrepreneurial, that we want to succeed … is also one of the things that make us … peculiarly gullible.".

It's hard to know whether to hate the man or admire him for his unfailing belief in a lie that he created, recreated and repackaged for most of his adult life. Fantasy or fraud, MacGregor made a success out of duping people to the extent that even his victims wanted to believe him despite the obvious truth in front of their eyes. Anyone fancy a trip to Poyais? I'm buying!

# Duer's Insider Trading Scam

Looking back on the history of Wall Street and the list of panics,

crises and depressions that start in that fateful place, you might imagine that
the street itself is cursed. You could suppose that, before the founding of
the colony of Manhattan, the area was an odious swamp. The natives would
give it a wide berth because they knew better; they knew that going near it
could cause their crops to fail or their children to be consumed by dread
ambition. But no - as with all great horror stories - the true horror was man.

Men built Wall Street, and men convinced the people of America and
then the world that Wall Street was too big to fail, and so it continues to
consolidate earnings into increasingly impressive and yet precarious towers,
despite the fact that it is obvious those towers will eventually fall. There is a
lot of evidence to support this hypothesis because it came close to failing
the year it opened. This is the story of the panic of 1792.

The U.S. financial crisis of 1792 is typically regarded as the first crash of the nascent American financial system. The U.S was a young country, and Wall Street was an even younger experiment, and it can be argued that if the panic hadn't happened in 1792, someone else would have eventually caused a crash similar in scope.

In 1792, the world was going through the last stages of a financial revolution. Joint stock companies and public debt in the form of bonds had been introduced at the end of the 1600s, and for a young nation like the United States, the establishment of a stock market was a natural evolution meeting the need to introduce methods which could help finance both private enterprise and the state itself.

Unlike earlier collapses, like France's Mississippi Bubble and England's South Sea Bubble, the panic of 1792 was dealt with effectively, and the actions that were taken ensured that the financial revolution continued to evolve and benefit the young nation.

Financial, industrial and political leaders of the day understood that ensuring stability in the capital markets would benefit the United States in many ways. They understood that as a result of the survival of the financial markets in the aftermath of the South Sea Bubble, the British Empire would go on to win all its wars, save one, between the years of 1688 and 1815. Great Britain would undergo an industrial revolution and, continuing to need to ship an ever-expanding population of convicts and Irish rabble, would go on to greatly expand its worldwide empire.

With the collapse of the Mississippi Bubble, France would have an altogether different experience. She would lose all her wars, would have a different sort of revolution than the industrial revolution featuring a regicidal and tyrannical period that would culminate with a dictatorship under Napoleon Bonaparte.

Ironically, the United States benefited from Bonaparte's arrival, when the latter decided to hold a fire sale of French territories by selling France's claims to the lands west of the Mississippi, including the territory of Louisiana, and the port of New Orleans. The Americans, fresh from their own successful revolution, were able to issue U.S. government bonds to the tune of 15 Million dollars to facilitate this transaction. Napoleon quickly sold these U.S. bonds to European and English investors and used the proceeds to gear up his war machine against Great Britain and her grand coalition.

The start of the Panic of 1792 began as financial panics usually do. Someone gets greedy and has an active imagination. In this case, a man named William Duer.

Duer was an American so long ago that he was actually an Englishman for the early years of his life. He was born in Devon County, Great Britain, in 1743, the son of John Duer, a planter of Antigua and Frances Frye, daughter of Sir Frederick Frye, who held a command in the West Indies. Like all silver spoon-fed children of the era, he studied at Eton, that prestigious academy for the training of history's future villains, and was promptly commissioned into the British army as an ensign, accompanying Robert Clive as aide-de-camp on his return to India as governor-general in 1762. Apparently, young Duer quickly tired of participating in the oppression of the Indian continent and, claiming that he couldn't handle the climate, he was shipped back home to England to his family's Devonshire estate.

Flouncing around England for a few years as a dilettante, he patiently waited for his father to die. As the third son, his Inheritance was not substantial, so he tried his hand at the family business and moved to Antigua, where he could oppress a whole different race of people.

Oppression was big business, and soon he was making regular trips to New York to trade his ill-gotten gains for whatever he could get. He made a trading partner and friend in Philip Schuyler who offered him slave-cut lumber for his slave-grown sugar cane. Their agreement was so lucrative that when Schuyler suggested Duer move to New York permanently, he jumped on a boat without question. He set up a new estate in Albany on the banks of the Hudson and soon opened sawmills and warehouses, along with a company store. By 1776, Duer had built a moderately successful mercantile business based primarily on slave-cut lumber. With his newly founded lumber operation, he went on to win contracts and sell ships' masts to the British Navy so that they could deliver better-armed oppression to the world. It was a different time. A simpler time. If you happened to be rich and white.

When the revolution rolled around, Duer didn't actually have that much against the British. He certainly wasn't there in Boston dumping tea into the ocean, but he ended up joining the New York Senate because all of his friends were doing it. Eventually, he became a member of the Continental Congress, a New York Judge, a good friend to Alexander Hamilton and even a signatory to the Articles of Confederation.

Now a proud American, he swapped his manufacturing contracts over to the American army. He made so much money in this period that he quit the Senate to be able to focus all his energy on managing his estates.

At this point, Duer's name was synonymous with that all-important quality of integrity in New York's elite circles. Integrity that was bought by being a member of the lucky sperm club otherwise known as the upper class. He resided just around the corner from Wall Street and married a bride who was given away by none other than George Washington himself. To describe Duer as a man with connections was an understatement.

Continuing his ascent into society, he accepted the job of Secretary to the Board of the Treasury, tasked with the oversight of financial and monetary matters, and it could be argued that this was where all his troubles began.

Toiling at the treasury for three years, Duer was well positioned to gain an insider's view of the young American financial system. In 1791 he resigned his position at the Treasury and entered into a partnership with a man by the name of Alexander Macomb, one of New York's wealthiest individuals.

While Duer was well known and generally liked by New York's elite, he was treated with suspicion by some important players of the time, like Thomas Jefferson. The main reason for the mistrust was that Duer was a speculator. Jefferson wrote to Washington in 1792: "All the capital employed in paper speculation is barren and useless, producing, like that on a gaming table, no accession to itself, and is withdrawn from commerce and agriculture where it would have produced an addition to the common mass. It nourishes in our citizens, habits of vice and idleness instead of industry and morality It has furnished effectual means of corrupting such a portion of the legislature as turns the balance between the honest voters whichever way it is directed."

Duer, at this point, had worked out that any stock being traded didn't need any actual value - it merely required a perceived value. That is to say, the emperor's new clothes can be wildly expensive when marketed in the right way. So he started trading stocks that were wildly expensive but had no relevant material worth.

Once that worthless stock had moved through a few more hands, it became very hard to trace back to Duer. It was a hot property, too, with everyone trying to get in on profit margins that seemed too good to be true, probably because they were. To consolidate this success, Duer founded the Scioto Company.

The Scioto Company, run by a team of agents that Duer hired to keep his own hands clean, claimed to own vast tracts of land in Ohio, which they sold in Paris to potential colonists of the New World. When those colonists arrived, they found their promised land didn't exist and were instead placed into interim housing. This housing was a series of crude huts in which they were told to wait until the Scioto Company had finalised its dealings. They were built on the only bit of land in Ohio that the Scioto Company actually did own.

That wasn't the end of the bad news for the tenants as they were then evicted once said land was returned to the ownership of the state of Ohio. The Scioto Company had failed to make its payments. It is hard to find any information on where those colonists were forced to go next. Hopefully, they made it back to Paris or found somewhere new to live in the United States. History, however, tells us it was quite common for colonists to disappear without a trace.

Returning to the speculation game and despite all the money he had made, he still resented having to pay a commission to the auctioneers who facilitated trades between himself and other business people. He was not alone in that. In fact, so many of the rich traders in New York at the time were frustrated by the commissions being charged on trades that they gathered together in their most formal powdered wigs under the shade of a buttonwood tree. There, on May 17th, 1792, they signed an agreement that formed the basis for the global stock market - probably to an ominous crack of thunder on an otherwise clear day. The buttonwood tree stood on Wall Street, and that agreement started the New York Stock Exchange.

Without the third party regulation of an auctioneer, it fell to the traders themselves to estimate how much their stock was worth. Speculation was a gamble, but one that paid off in unprecedented wealth for those who estimated correctly. As trades progressed, however, it became harder and harder for the players involved to know when to get off the merry-go-round and leave the last man "holding the bag."

Speculation made Duer a wealthy man. Seeing this success as a sign of Duer's considerable financial expertise, Alexander Hamilton offered him a job. Hamilton, in addition to being a founding father and treasurer of the United States, was also the son-in-law of Duer's dear friend Philip Schuyler. He appointed Duer as the chief salesman of the Society for Establishing Useful Manufactures. Otherwise referred to as SUM. Of course, Duer took this as another opportunity to make as much money as possible with little regard for the consequences of his actions.

Using Macomb's money as a springboard and his knowledge of the financial system from his stint as the secretary to the treasury, he used the SUM as an excuse to start fundraising from whoever he could, building up a debt of almost $300,000, most of which was owned by the Bank of America. He began to speculate on the New York bank's stock. The New York bank was the first company to be traded on Wall Street, and today it would be considered a Blue Chip company. At this point, people began to take notice. New York Governor George Clinton and Thomas Jefferson himself began to work to expose Duer. Jefferson had been opposed to the appointment of Alexander Hamilton and the whole idea of a Bank of America in the first place, so he saw this as his opportunity to prove them both wrong. Clinton had his allies withdraw huge amounts from the Bank of America to try to force a credit shortage.

Acting in parallel, others had an active interest in seeing New York Bank's stock prices fall, namely the Livingstons, one of the wealthiest families in New York. To facilitate the fall in prices, they began a coordinated withdrawal of gold and silver from the New York Bank deposits, which had the effect of contracting the banks' local money supply. The banks were forced to call in loans to ensure their solvency, and this instituted a credit squeeze. Interest rates spiked to as much as one per cent a day. This quickly became ruinous for Duer and others who had borrowed massively to continue their speculative activities.

Desperation ensued, and he tried to borrow money to cover his obligations, but the gig was up. No one was willing to lend and be left holding the bag. Along with the actions of Duer, this credit-fueled speculative bubble pushed the credit system to the breaking point. So began the Panic of 1792. Immediately, Duer was thrown in debtor's prison where he joined Macomb and some other associates.

The Panic created widespread famine and left the Bank of America and many other banks close to failure. The United States of America was almost bankrupt and close to implosion less than two decades after it was born. You would imagine the New York Stock Exchange would have been written off as a bad idea at that point, but Alexander Hamilton swooped in to save the day. Riding to the rescue, he ensured that the country's financial system didn't collapse. He ordered the Treasury to mop up the liquidity in the market by purchasing several hundred thousand dollars' worth of federal securities to support the prices. He had browbeaten the banks into ceasing their loan calls and calm quickly returned. Hamilton later used his influence to convince the nation's few and mostly new banks to restrict credit in order to prevent new bubbles from starting in the first place.

This founding father started a tradition that is still celebrated about once every ten to twenty years in America: he kept the banks from collapsing by providing them with huge bailouts of public funds, using the people's money to pay for the crimes of the super-rich. This is perhaps why he is now celebrated as a national hero on Broadway.

Duer lived out the rest of his life in prison and died there in 1799. Thomas Jefferson went on to become the third president of the United States. Alexander Hamilton was killed in a duel.

In quietly serving out his life sentence, Duer may have escaped mainstream infamy, but his legacy lives on in the spirit of the stock exchange to this day. In the ensuing investigation, Duer was found to have executed so many trades on inside information that he became the first to be known to do so by a widespread audience. Shortly after the collapse, about a month later, the auctioneers and dealers, those people that were despised by Duer and his associates, decided that they had best move their operations in from the street and coffee houses. They realised that, in order to keep public opinion on their side, they needed a facade of credibility and to establish their operation in a central location. This move would greatly improve control mechanisms that would later follow and allow for better record keeping.

Historians generally agree that there was little fallout from the panic of 1792. The Nation's industrial production and Gross Domestic Product grew every year from 1790 to 1796. The nascent market and banks stabilised in April of that year, and the nation did not experience another bank failure for another 18 years.

Looking back to Alan Greenspan's actions of recent decades, it is apparent that Greenspan prevented several potentially similar collapses of the securities market and bond markets. He is credited with preventing a larger scale crash in 1987, diminishing the effect of the dot.com bubble after 1999, and calming markets after the September 11th 2001 terrorist attacks from having any major negative effects for the US economy.

Alexander Hamilton in 1791 and 1792 did not have the benefit of Greenspan's hindsight. He could not draw upon a history of managing a financial crisis. Instead, he had to 'Wing it' and roll the dice with his decisions, in what can be only regarded as a stroke of genius. His greatest success was saving the financial revolution and enhancing the economic and political power of the young nation.

The 2008 global financial crisis was caused by traders packaging reliable mortgages with greater and greater proportions of toxic, unpayable debt and allowing people to sign financial agreements that would damn them to bankruptcy with their impossible interest rates. The crisis was ended by the provision of huge amounts of public funds the world over creating a recession that can still be felt today. What's worse is that many of those traders weren't imprisoned like William Duer and they are still working on Wall Street, sowing the seeds of the next financial disaster.

# LOU BLONGER AND THE 'BIG CON'

In 1922, Herbert Grey, an Englishman, was visiting Denver on business when he was approached by a friendly stranger who called himself Webb. Grey was alone, watching a fly fishing competition to while away a spare summers evening, and he was grateful for the pleasant company. They went for dinner at a restaurant that Webb recommended, and Webb offered to show him the sights over the weekend. It seemed Grey had found himself the perfect tour guide. They would go on regular road trips and, before long; Grey was spending most evenings with Webb and getting to know his circle of friends. Many of them were wealthy and threw lavish parties where the champagne flowed freely despite the strict prohibition laws at the time. At one such party, probably after a couple of glasses of fine wine, Grey was introduced to an unassuming man named Reynolds. Reynolds was defensive at first, confused as to why he was being approached, all-too-aware of what he was famous for, but he was susceptible to a few compliments from Webb and the general atmosphere of conspiratorial bonheur.

"You just want me for my money," Reynolds joked with them. "You know you could easily make it yourselves? "He had reportedly made $25,000 on the stock market in just a few weeks. Adjusting for inflation, that would be closer to $300,000 today. That may not seem like much in comparison to some of the takings that traders make on the modern stock market, but that's a scam for another day. It was a lot of money. It was certainly enough to pique the interest of Grey and Webb. Reynolds told them he had some insider knowledge on the stock market. He could help them make a few investments if they wanted, and he would only take a very modest commission. Of course, it wasn't without risk, but his tips were as close to certain as you could get in the exciting new world of finance.

The next morning, still nursing his hangover and not restored to the height of his mental faculties, Grey was driven over to the stock exchange in the Denham Building. Tentative, and wishing he could be sat over a plate of eggs instead, he placed his first investment: a modest $20. When Reynolds returned with $40 after just a few minutes trading, Grey started to feel a lot better. Perhaps he would have steak with his eggs. And a glass of champagne.

Soon that $20 was closer to $1000, and Grey was elated with the thrill of cheating the system. No longer would he have to make the arduous journey across the Atlantic and away from his loving family for months on end just to make his sales. He could finally buy that cottage on an estate out in the countryside and have a pair of cocker spaniels and spend his afternoons walking his land hunting grouse with a shotgun.

"What's the largest amount I can invest on credit?" he asked, to which his new friends exchanged a smile. Grey took that smile to mean that they were proud that their timid acquaintance was slipping into the spirit of the Land of Opportunity. He couldn't have been more wrong.

The trade of $25,000 took quite a bit longer this time. Webb persuaded Grey to come with him for some breakfast in the meantime and, although Grey was reluctant to leave the dreams of his future untended, the desire for eggs prevailed. When they returned, Reynolds was stacking Grey's huge takings into a suitcase. He put the weighty suitcase into Grey's hands, and Grey was heading for the door to telegram his wife the good news before the owner of the exchange stopped him and pointed out that he had made those trades on credit. The money was his to take if he could just present them with the original $25,000. He was given time to return to England to gather the funds. This took the wind out of his sails somewhat, so it was fortunate that his boat home was steam powered.

When he returned to England, he and his wife began to muse on all the wonderful things they could buy with the money. They looked into cottages in the country. Jumping the gun, Grey even bought his wife an extravagant fur coat. It wasn't long before their dreams had outgrown the amount of money he had won, so when he returned to Denver and paid his credit and Reynolds proposed one last trade before they sign to make it all official, Grey leapt at the prospect. That was to be his undoing. Reynolds lost all of the money and had to come back to Grey, hat in hand, promising to repay his initial investment. Reynolds took Grey for a conciliatory meal.

Over their coffee, into which Reynolds had poured whisky from his flask with a wink, he said:

"Listen, Grey, I haven't been totally upfront with you. It wouldn't have been an issue had this all gone to plan, but there was always a risk, and I should have just told you in the first place. My mother always told me I was a fool and that I'd meet a fool's end. The trading, it wasn't entirely… above board."

"Excuse me, sir, but what exactly are you saying?" Grey asked, boiling over with the terse politeness of an enraged Englishman. "There was a reason all the trades went so well. It was meant to be foolproof. I guess I'm the fool they should use to test these things. If my employer finds out, it'll be jail for both of us."

Grey spat his coffee in a most un-English fashion. "Jail?"

"Maybe the rope for me," said Reynolds. He puffed on his cigarette. "Look, they won't catch me. It's going to be fine. You just head back to England in the morning and wait for my telegram. I'll meet you in London with the money. We can go see that big clock you all love so much."

There wasn't any more to say. Grey left for the safety of England the next morning, thinking every noise behind him was the approach of a sheriff's boots. He was safely home for months before he realised Reynolds wasn't coming. At that point, he sent a telegram to the Denver district attorney.

This was not the first time the district attorney had heard troubling news like this from Denver. Recently elected to his post, Philip Van Cise was a fastidious man, meticulous with details, and so this news was especially troubling to him because there were so many details missing. But, as he agonised over his notes, pinning them to a corkboard and linking them with red string, his phone rang. It was Denver police chief Hamilton Armstrong giving Van Cise the name that would sit at the centre of his red string web: Lou Blonger.

Lou Blonger was a French Canadian immigrant who had come to Denver as a teen and climbed his way up to managing a nightclub. He was also a master of extortion and bribery, a pioneer in wiretapping technology. Well aware of the power of information, and working in the kind of place that people go to make dirty secrets, Blonger had secured himself a network of crooked cops and government officials. Holding an envelope of incriminating photographs over the heads of so many authority figures, he had been able to offer protection to those criminal elements in Denver that were successful enough to pay for it. Of course, he had information on them, too.

With Blonger's racket in place, Denver became a hotbed for all kinds of confidence games. There was barely a legitimate business left in the place though, with all the officials compromised, it still gave off the outward appearance of normalcy - even one of opulence. It was a scammer's paradise. Almost every person Grey had met while being taken for a ride was in on it. Webb led him to Reynolds who led him to the manager of the stock exchange. The stock exchange itself was an elaborate front that snared hundreds of victims, and none for less than $5000. Blonger's final takings were estimated to be in the millions. Armstrong was desperate. He was one of the only honest cops in a city running wild with crime. There were corrupt detectives hiding evidence, tipping off perps before Armstrong could arrive with the few cops he knew he could trust, and Armstrong couldn't even fire them because even the governor was in Blonger's pocket. There was nothing he could do but walk the streets and scowl at the buildings he knew were fronts for bars or brothels. That was why he reached out to the district attorney. What followed was a war of information in Denver. Some of those Armstrong thought he could trust fell under Blonger's influence, but there were also many who wanted Blonger gone before their secrets could be revealed and, on top of that, plenty of innocent townsfolk who just weren't fond of the rising presence of organised crime in their area. He even got Blonger's postman and janitor onside, so he knew everything that came in, and out, of Blonger's office.

Everyone was watching everyone, the names of Van Cise and Blonger were on every pair of lips, but Van Cise was canny enough to not reveal his plan before it was time to put it into action and, in starting the war of information, he gained a sense of who he could trust when he finally came to town.

The preparations took over a year. The investigation was so protracted it nearly failed due to budget concerns. By this point, the people of Denver were so tired of Blonger's hand in their pockets that they turned out their pockets themselves to help fund the operation. This way they only had to pay once.

The operation had to happen all on the same day so that none of Blonger's ring had time to escape. On the day in question, there was a curious sight at the First Universalist Church on E. Colefax Avenue. A regular civilian car pulled up outside. From it emerged two regular civilians leading a hardened criminal in handcuffs. They took the man inside. Then another car showed up, and the same thing happened. Then it happened again, and again. It wasn't long before Blonger himself showed up, also in handcuffs. Van Cise made a point of putting him at the front of the list of arrests so that no one could tip him off. By lunchtime, the church was filled with bemused, irate con men in handcuffs. It was a raging success. Through cooperation with the local community, Van Cise was able to overthrow the entire Blonger ring and release Denver from their insidious clutches. While awaiting trial, Blonger made numerous attempts to have his associates compromise the integrity of Van Cise and Armstrong. He even once tried to send a beautiful escort to seduce Van Cise, but, as a sign of how far Blonger had fallen, the escort just took Blonger's money and ran. He was sentenced to seven years in prison but, perhaps as one last way of cheating the system, he died after just five months.

# THE PROTOCOLS OF THE ELDERS OF ZION FORGERY

There are lots of scams, from pyramid schemes to card tricks; from bank frauds to religious swindles. There is still plenty of plagiarism, despite the efforts of writers and legal institutions around the world. Conspiracy theories are abundant, especially if you venture into the uncharted waters of the conspiracy community that lurks in the depths of virtual reality. The special thing about The Protocols of the Elders of Zion is that it manages to combine all three in a trio of racial hatred, political paranoia and media machinations. To gain a more in-depth understanding of The Protocols, what they were, where they came from and what they have come to mean over the years, it's important to examine them in the context of each of their constructs – as a scam, as an act of plagiarism and as a conspiracy theory.

The Protocols of Zion purport to contain the minutes from a series of twenty-four meetings attended by the leading Jewish thinkers of the time.

The meetings are supposedly discussions on how to control non-Jews and unknowingly turn them into slaves of the Jewish people who can then be controlled as Jews take over institutions across the world. In a way, we should be grateful that such a document emerged only before the establishment of the internet which would have accelerated their dissemination beyond belief, although the development of the rotary printing press in the early 20th century certainly facilitated the anti-Semites in circulating the document far and wide. Even today, when browsing the virtual world for information about The Protocols, a whole range of sites can be found both denying their validity and stating a case for their authenticity and their continued relevance. This makes The Protocols scam one of the longest-running and influential in modern times.

A scam is a method of securing something of worth, such as money, power or influence, by tricking an individual, company or group of people into believing something that isn't true. The strange thing about The Protocols of Zion is that it wasn't going to make anyone rich, unless, of course, its content was true, in which case, the Jews were going to take over the world's wealth through a series of underhand methods.

Conspiracy theories abound in modern society, including everything from religion to space travel and from the murder of John F Kennedy to the 9/11 attacks, but one of the most enduring is the notion that a group of elite people is controlling the world. This concept has been around for centuries, and there is no evidence that the end is in sight. The philosophy suggests that this secret group aims, eventually, to create a New World

Order which will enable them to dissolve boundaries between nations and establish themselves as the totalitarian authority in charge of the whole world.

Plagiarism sounds rather tame by comparison but, in fact, is an act of fraud. The presentation of someone else's work as one's own is not only a grave act of misconduct but is also deceptive – the theft of someone's words or ideas can have serious consequences. One only has to look as far as the recent debacle over Melania Trump's speech at the Republican National Convention to understand that!

While many scams are about making money, most conspiracy theories are centred on power and the misuse thereof. Literary plagiarism is often motivated by an inability to create something quite as impressive as that written by a rival author. The Protocols of Zion is a strange combination of all three and, it would appear, rather than being prompted by greed for money, it was spurred on by a desire for power and hatred of a deep and provoking nature – racial hatred. Animosity towards anyone who is unlike ourselves in our tribal minds has been going on since the first humans discovered the art of war and continues even as we evolve into a predominantly virtual world. In fact, the connectivity inspired by the world wide web has facilitated further antagonism or at least enabled people to connect across the globe in their bitterness and acrimony.

While anti-Semitism is perceived to have reached its zenith under Nazi rule in German, this scam predated Hitler by nearly 30 years and continues to circulate today, which serves to prove the need humans feel to have an enemy in the opposing corner. So much of our understanding of ourselves and our world is structured around polar opposites that, if the opposite isn't there, make little real sense. Can we have white if we don't have black? Can there be a woman if there isn't a man? Can Trump be President if there isn't a dark "other", such as Islamic extremists, threatening American identity and unity?

Allegedly leaked from France in the late 1800s, The Protocols of the Elders of Zion was first published in 1903, shortly before the Russian Revolution, and was declared to be a true document detailing the plans Jewish leaders were making for world domination. While it sounds like something out of a James Bond movie, this is far more divisive and inflammatory than any fictional plot from the mind of Ian Fleming. 500,000 copies of the document hit the US in the 1920s, funded by motorcar mogul Henry Ford, who initially published the articles in his newspaper, The Dearborn Independent. Upon publication, Ford declared: "The only statement I care to make about The Protocols is that they fit in with what is going on. They are 16 years old, and they have fitted the world situation up to this time." Ford subsequently published a series of books which contained both The Protocols articles, in addition to other material of a similar nature. Some years later, in 1927, Ford was pressured to make another statement in which he apologised for the publication and retracted his previous statement.

In a sense, however, the damage had already been done – the document was out there for people to read and develop their own considerations about its origins and authenticity. Alfred Rosenberg, an influential member of the Nazi Party, showed the document to Adolf Hitler who went on to quote from it on many occasions. Containing declarations such as how the Jews will infiltrate and dominate international media organisations while, themselves, remaining completely anonymous, The Protocols creates the image of an invisible evil that infiltrates every corner of our civilised world. According to Norman Cohn, once in the hands (and minds) of the Nazis, it became a "Warrant for Genocide". After all, an invisible, insidious evil cannot be fought in a duel nor a war, but must be either forced out of hiding or simply destroyed in every corner it could possibly exist in. The Protocols provided the Nazis with a manual that justified their hatred and affirmed for them that the only way to deal with the Jewish threat was to eliminate it completely, thus leading to the devastating Holocaust which cost millions of lives.


One of the most famous examples of literary forgery in the world, the discussions surrounding The Protocols has been going on since its original release. The document itself details, with the use of all-consuming banalities and clichés, how the Jews planned to change the social order by taking over media and financial institutions across the world. In other words, it follows precisely the popular conspiracy theory that a secret elite is planning to take over the world and control it in an authoritarian manner. Many Jews are in positions of power within international media companies, financial bodies and judicial organisations, and some may perceive this to be evidence that the plans laid out in The Protocols are coming to fruition. Others might just assert that there are well-educated people out there in positions of power which they have secured through their education, experience and know-how who also happen to be Jewish. Just as there are people in influential positions throughout the world, who are not Jewish. Not a conspiracy – just a representation of the different cultures, belief systems and religions in existence.

The cultural context of the original release of The Protocols is telling; not only had the Russians lost face and land in the war against Japan, but they had also compromised their country's industrialisation with their recklessness in war. Poor living conditions, high taxes and the hunger for land ownership had brought considerable unrest and hardship. The Protocols blamed the Jews for all these negative influences. Wielded as a political weapon aimed at destroying the Bolsheviks, who were seen to be primarily Jewish, The Protocols' purpose was to discredit the revolution, dissuade the West from recognising the Soviet Union and destroy Lenin's regime.

It is argued that the original document was produced as a parody of Jewish idealism and was meant only for internal circulation. In fact, the original document's source has been given so many different names and faces over the years that it can be perceived as a literary hall of mirrors. Even its original publication is unclear, with some claiming it first appears as a commentary on a book entitled The Great in Little – The Coming of the Antichrist and the Rule of Satan, penned by Sergei Nilus. Others assert that the document first came to light in a series of articles published by a newspaper called Znamya (The Banner). Regardless of where and when it first appeared, it seems the motivation behind the document was to impress a rather feeble-minded Russian Czar that those who were against him, such as the Jews, whom he hated, were also against Christ. If not held in check, they would wrest the most powerful positions away from God-fearing Christians and hand the entire civilised world over to the Antichrist. This belief is reiterated on numerous conspiracy sites all over the internet.

These sites contain some bizarre and rather mind-boggling theories relating to The Protocols. According to a document published on a site that calls itself Three World Wars, The Protocols is not a plan for Jewish world domination but rather a grand plan to create a New World Order written by "supernatural Guiding Spirits through Automatic Writing". That clears that up then!

Over the years, Sergei Nilus identified some ever-changing and contradictory sources. In 1905 he claimed The Protocols were leaked from a secret meeting of leading Freemasonry representatives held in France. Later, he said he had stolen them himself from a French headquarters of the Society of Zion. Still, later, he admitted that the documents weren't of French origin at all, but came from Switzerland where they had formed part of documents secretly read at a Zionist Congress held in Basle in 1897. What is true is that this conference took place and was the first international Zionist meeting. What is completely false is that it was a secret meeting which only the most elite Jewish thinkers could attend. In fact, the conference was attended by several Christians as well as media representatives and was widely covered in the European and American newspapers. Strange, then, to think that a completely secret document emerged from this meeting.

According to media coverage and historical documents detailing the events of the Congress, the Zionist Organization was formed during the meeting; the Hatikvah was adopted as its anthem and plans were laid out regarding the establishment of a safe home for Jewish people in Palestine. Doesn't really coincide with the concept of world domination and the takeover of all gentile institutions in the effort to create a New World Order, does it? Or am I missing something? Although anti-Semitic believers attest that The Protocols forms a blueprint of the Jewish plan for world domination, in fact, most of the ideas put forward within the document were already widely circulated. In a time of political unrest, many people and writers were discussing suspicions that the politicians of the era were dishonest and power-hungry. Some things simply don't change. In effect, that also meant they were open to manipulation if it meant their own political aspirations would be achieved. Some other things don't change either!

Upon its arrival in England, The Protocols was initially favourably received with *The Times* attesting to its prophetic significance. According to *The Times* in May 1920, the real threats to the world and its Christian values were not coming from Germany but rather from the Jews. Wickham Steed, then Chief Editor of *The Times*, was known for his tendency towards anti-Semitism, so it came as no surprise that the paper published an editorial endorsing The Protocols as a genuine document. The editorial asked, "Are they forgery? If so, whence comes the uncanny note of prophecy, in part fulfilled, in the past so far gone in the way of fulfilment?"

A year later, *The Times* changed its tune with Constantinople correspondent, Philip Graves, stating that The Protocols hadn't been written by a secret Jewish source at all and casting doubt on the authenticity of the document. According to Graves, the source of The Protocols' content was provided to him by a Russian émigré who was reluctant to be named but who wanted the information exposed in order not to "give a weapon of any kind to the Jews, whose friend I have never been." The Russian was later identified as Michael Raslovelef, and Graves' first article asserted that The Protocols was "in the main a clumsy plagiarism" of a book written by Frenchman Maurice Joly in 1864. Joly's Dialogue in Hell between Machiavelli and Montesquieu attacked Napoleon III, and The Protocols contained no fewer than one hundred and sixty passages lifted directly from this manuscript. By coincidence, Joly's original manuscript was far from unique itself and was largely lifted from a previous publication entitled Les Mystères du Peuple, written by Eugène Sue. Although Herman Bernstein in the US also produced an entire book about the hoax in the same year, The Protocols continued to be widely regarded as both important and factual.

Although those who were convinced of The Protocols legacy and pursued the distribution of these documents could not agree on their origin, they continued to proclaim their authenticity. Nilus produced a second edition of the documents in 1917 but the revolution which took place in Russia in the same year put a more liberal mind in charge of the country and resulted in the destruction of the newly released Protocols. Nilus was arrested and punished for causing "incalculable harm" through the publication. Imprisoned and tortured, Nilus subsequently died in exile in 1929. Nevertheless, a couple of copies of the re-released Protocols were salvaged and published in many countries, including Germany, England and America. Despite this international vote of confidence, there was nothing within the documents that showed any consistency with Jewish history or the religions' philosophies of the times.

Nilus claimed that The Protocols had come to him from a man by the name of Piotr Ivan Ratchkovsky, a secret policeman who headed up a French branch of Okhrana (the KGB's predecessor). In turn, it seems, Ratchkovsky had asked a man by the name of Golovinski to pen the text in 1897 for Ratchkovsky's own political gain. As the head of the Paris branch of the Okhrana, Ratchkovsky was eager to accelerate his political career but had his nose put somewhat out of joint by policy-maker Sergei Witte. Witte had established himself to the extent that he wielded great influence over the Czar and Ratchkovsky saw The Protocols transcript as an opportunity to out-Witte him and gain the Czar's attention and respect.

The Protocols, in this instance, took a very similar position to Joly's original satirical text. Joly had set out to show the conflict between a dictatorial style of leadership and a more democratic view and, in a rather bizarre turn of events, The Protocols ended up as a weapon in the battle between those who supported the current absolutist regime and those who wanted reform. According to American historian, writer, and commentator, Daniel Pipes, The Protocols' real significance lies in its ability to reach beyond the limited circles of anti-Semites to influence a larger international audience and convince them of its authenticity. The Protocols is suitably vague, and this lack of detail assists it in appealing to people across the board, regardless of class, religion and culture. Emphasising recurrent conspiracy theory themes, The Protocols highlights the notion of a shadowy enemy who is ever-present but moves unseen through the most influential establishments in the world.

In 1934, The Protocols hit the headlines once more but this time in faraway Africa. A South African court case brought by Rev. A Levy against three notorious Grey Shirts, Henry Victor Inch, Johannes von Strauss von Moltke and David Hormanns Olivier found in favour of the plaintiff and fined the three accused. In his summation of the case, Justice Gutsch stated that "Israel has no secret protocols, no hidden designs. Its dream is still of peace, of justice and of human brotherhood... The Holy Scriptures are the only authentic Protocols of the Wise Men of Zion."

Inevitably, The Protocols fell into Nazi hands and added fuel to their anti-Semitic fire despite conclusive proof that they were a complete fabrication. Following the disastrous First World War, The Protocols were put forward as a valid explanation for all Germany's problems, from the hunger and devastating inflation to failure to win the war. Is this ringing some bells? Remember The Protocols was initially written to support a failing regime in a country beset by failure in conflict and high taxes! In Mein Kampf, Hitler claims that, despite assertions as to their forged status, "they reveal the nature and activity of the Jewish people and expose... their ultimate final aims."

Despite the longevity of the evidence against the authenticity of The Protocols, leaders of Arab and Muslim regimes in the Middle East continue to endorse them. As recently as 2005, a new edition of The Protocols was authorised by the Syrian Ministry of Information which includes what purports to be an "investigative" study that indicates that the Torah and Talmud incite Jews "to commit treason and to conspire, dominate, be arrogant and exploit other countries." In 2006, The Protocols continued to form a part of the curriculum in Saudi Arabia, and a textbook for boys contains a section on the Zionist Movement in which The Protocols is presented as an authentic document designed to teach students that the Jews are responsible for much of the world's dissonance and conflict.

Throughout The Protocols' tumultuous history in the US, the concept of Jewish control over the media has been one of the most controversial ideas of its time. Within the plagiarised document, there are some references to the power of the press and one excerpt claims: "The Press have gained the power to influence while remaining ourselves in the shade; thanks to the Press we have got the GOLD in our hands... The Press, which, with a few exceptions that may be disregarded, is already entirely in our hands."

Given the number of Jews holding influential positions in all industries, from medical to media, political to industrial, it could be suggested that, if world domination were truly their aim, they would have achieved it by now, especially if they had really been planning the takeover since 1905! The few specifics that are written into The Protocols provide further evidence of their absurdity. According to one extract, the Jews were planning to hide explosives under various power-wielding Gentile cities around the world. The explosives would be placed in the underground railway systems and used to destabilise the Western world. Evidently, the Jews wrote this specifically to keep their real plans – of airborne bombings – secret from the rest of the world!

According to Edward Rothstein in his New York Times article published in 2006, the power of The Protocols comes from it finding resonance with many different belief systems across the world. He claims that the anti-Semites who hold the document to be true do so, in part, "...because, in its villainous Jews, they see images of what they yearn to be." It is arguable that The Protocols is as applicable to America's desire to disseminate its cultural beliefs across the world with globalisation as it is to any theoretical underground Jewish movement.

The fact that The Protocols shares so much in common with Joly's Dialogues in Hell between Machiavelli and Montesquieu is the basis of the evidence supporting the claim that it is plagiarised. As a lawyer, Joly set about writing Dialogues in Hell as a critique of Napoleon III's dictatorship and used two characters to represent opposing opinions on the politics of the time. Montesquieu represents policies of force, while Machiavelli is the spokesperson for policies of justice. Other inconsistencies arise from the content of The Protocols, particularly the reference to the French Revolution in the third Protocol which states, "... the secrets of its preparations are well known to us, for it was wholly the work of our hands." Given that the few Jews present in France at the time had no political rights, they did not play a significant role in the revolution. As the name "French Revolution", this period of upheaval was actually instigated by none other than the French.

The language used in The Protocols is the same as that used within many conspiracy theory texts, regardless of who the source of evil is meant to be. The notion that the populace will be distracted by money, sport, fame and fortune, while a handful of cunning and influential individuals secure power for themselves is consistent throughout conspiracy narratives.

Unfortunately, many people believe what they read without considering its origins, in a range of different contexts. Take, for example, those who, on a visit to their doctor, tell their educated, trained professional that they "know" they have a certain condition because they read about it on the internet. Unfortunately, it is very easy to make connections that do not exist based on the assumption that what we have read is the absolute truth. Conspiracy theories use this strange tendency by operating as an organising tool for those who believe that someone else has the upper hand due to unfair advantages which have left them wanting. By identifying a random 'other' who has had opportunities unavailable to the masses, it's possible to ignite anger and galvanise the populace to action.

The temptation to believe in scams and conspiracy theories comes from an underlying desire for power and the sense that that power has been unfairly distributed on the basis of money, class, gender, race or religion. Of course, knowing this weakness exists means that those who are wielding power, or are campaigning to reach a position of power, can exploit it quite easily. After all, Trump's campaign is case in point. Look at the image of a star of David, combined with Hillary Clinton's face and a pile of money which was tweeted during Trump's campaign. The picture says a thousand words – namely, that there is a shadowy caucus of international elites (many of whom happen to be Jewish) who are holding all the power.

Trump's concept of "fake news" sits in uncomfortable harmony with the conspiracy that leads to the creation of The Protocols. One only has to look at his claim that, "Any negative polls are fake news, just like the CNN, ABC, NBC polls in the election." Just as the Protocols twisted a satirical text into one centred on world domination, so the political spinners of today can turn fact into fiction and vice versa. In a statement issued by the White House on Holocaust Day, there was no mention of the Jews at all. When confronted about this, spokespeople claimed they merely wanted to assert that people from other religious groups and cultural backgrounds also lost their lives. This is surely missing the point. As much as we might want to rewrite history, we really can't. Sadly, the history of The Protocols of the Elders of Zion has made it startlingly apparent that lies have considerable staying power and the capacity to spur people into action and even wipe out entire populations. The pen, truly, is mightier than the sword.

# THE GREAT H2O GAS HOAX

Science is a peculiar thing, but scientists are more peculiar still. One only has to look at Albert Einstein's hair to get an idea of the crazy side that often fuels genius in the science sector. In fact, Einstein is probably one of the saner representatives of his profession, especially when compared to some self-proclaimed inventors. Inventors are notoriously special and, to give an idea of just how special, let's take a look at Canadian inventor John Hutchison. In the late 1970s, Hutchison claimed to be able to create certain frequencies that could shield gravity and make all sorts of elements levitate, including heavy metals. Hutchison has produced a vast collection of videos which he claims prove his incredible discoveries, although sceptics cast doubt on this evidence and speculated that the items that appeared to fly or levitate were really being pulled upward on strings. Another film showing ice cream levitating out of a cup also encountered doubt as non-believers suggested that the ice cream was, in fact, falling in front of an upended camera. Of course, it wasn't a string pulling the item into the air; rather, according to Hutchison, "The string is not a string but #32-gauge double poly thermalised wire on a take-up up reel with 20 to 50000 volts DC." So that clears that up then.

Unfortunately for Hutchison, the experiments proved somewhat difficult to reproduce and, to this day, the only evidence remains on tape. According to Hutchison, these niggles in the system are purely due to government intervention. Hutchison claimed much of his evidence was destroyed by the Canadian government after he refused to sign an agreement with them. Hutchison is still alive and well and has a whole website dedicated to the Hutchison effect. Another website purports to prove how technology related to Hutchison's discoveries was used to destroy the World Trade Centre on 9/11.

Hutchison is by no means on his own out there in the world of crazy science and one area that has attracted both crazy and educated inventors for the past hundred years or so is the creation of an alternative to petrol. There have been those who claim to run cars on compressed-air (this is, in fact, possible), while a Texan dog trainer invented the Pooch Mobile in 1939 which operates much like a hamster wheel, only with a dog in the wheel and a strange kind of bicycle construction in front. Alternatively, you could attach a massive bag of gas to the roof of your car and run it that way, as they did in China to reduce the running costs of buses. There are even claims that a car can be run on tequila alone – a notion that might lead to an interesting night out and a few regrets the morning after. Nevertheless, as strange as some of these alternatives may appear, some of them do work.

One of the key stumbling blocks for many inventors and chemists looking for new ways to run a car engine is their fundamental ignorance of how a car actually operates. Fortunately for them, this lack of knowledge is shared with many of the people they are trying to convince, which makes the motoring industry a prime target for all sorts of elaborate hoaxes and outrageous claims. A major car manufacturer is reported to have attended a conference on global warming at which an electric van was being displayed. Although the van had a completely normal car engine, powered by petrol, the ingenious creators had the foresight to paint the words, "Electric Van" on the side which was, apparently, enough to convince many of those attending the conference. So, while technology may have improved, intelligence hasn't necessarily kept up.

Water-powered engines are something of a unicorn in the car industry, and there have been many that had claimed to have produced an engine that can run solely on water – an idea that perhaps carried a little more weight before global warming started to threaten the water supplies on Earth. While finding alternatives to fossil fuels isn't a recent development, the search has intensified in light of environmental concerns and diminishing supplies of natural resources. In the Seventies, Sam Lesley Leach announced that he had found a way to liberate hydrogen from water and, in doing so, run a car on water alone. Unfortunately, the laws of thermodynamics got in the way… but more about that later. Leach was subsequently found guilty of fraud before dying, either from an aneurysm, as diagnosed by the coroner, or by poison, as claimed by a wholly reliable website dedicated to such underground information.

Wars, in particular, have always meant restrictions on fuels which have resulted in inflated costs and limited supplies. It was in these circumstances, during the First World War, that US inventor Louis Enricht first pitched his concept of a water-based alternative to gasoline. He was the first of many, and new inventions are still popping out of the woodwork regularly today, with the most recent reported attempt being made by Agha Waqar Ahmad in 2012. It's an understandable dream and, in 1916, the announcement that Enricht's alternative fuel could be bought for just 1c or 2c per gallon, compared to the 28c per gallon consumers were paying for petrol, was music to their ears and the unsuspecting public began to celebrate this genius's solution to a worldwide problem.

With gasoline in short supply because of the war, news of Louis Enricht's claims to have found a cheap and easily available alternative spread like wildfire, sending the automobile industry into a state of panic or excitement depending on your perspective. Rich businessmen are rarely willing to acknowledge inventions that might jeopardise their absolute rule but, then again, cheaper fuel might mean more people could afford to run cars which would surely be worth celebrating. Louis Enricht seems an unlikely candidate for such a momentous breakthrough. A gaunt man of German descent with a serious moustache, Enricht was perceived by his neighbours to be an eccentric and unproductive inventor. Already in his 70s and living in a dilapidated home, Louis Enricht appeared on the public scene with the announcement (made by all accounts in a rather trembling voice) that he had learned "to do what chemists have been dreaming of for years" and developed a unique formula. When added to water, this formula could run a combustion engine as efficiently as petrol. Unsurprisingly, the press and those with a vested interest in the automobile business were intrigued, if a little dubious. Consequently, when Enricht invited the press and other interested parties to attend a demonstration of his invention, he attracted a fair amount of attention. Among the attendants were a gaggle of newspapermen as well as Dr Miller Reese Hutchison (not to be confused with the Hutchison of the Hutchison Effect), an inventor who worked as the chief engineer for Thomas A. Edison and was asked to report back to Hudson Maxim of Maxim Munitions Corporation Company on the validity of Enricht's invention.

A noteworthy performance followed during which Enricht invited the gathered reporters to make a thorough examination of the vehicle to confirm there was no residual fuel in the tanks and no hidden auxiliary tanks that might influence the results. Enricht even invited one of the reporters to try and crank the engine which he did to no avail, informing the gathered crowd that it would not turn over as the gas gauge indicated an empty tank.

Once this initial inspection was complete, Enricht asked another of the onlookers to fill a bucket from a nearby hosepipe and then taste it, thus proving it was only water. At this point, the inventor was playing his audience like a well-loved fiddle, employing techniques like those used by magicians to misdirect perception. But, at this point, Enricht's claims and demonstration were completely truthful and above-board. Once the bucket of water was in his hands, Enricht pulled out a tube of green liquid, added two ounces of the solution to the water and then poured the resultant fluid into the vehicle's tank and cranked the engine. Much to the surprise of Dr Hutchison and, presumably, some other members of the gathered crowd, the engine turned over and ran smoothly. Enricht drove a few of the assembled crowd around for a couple of minutes and then returned home to wait for the flood of investments he anticipated would result from his successful demonstration.

Enricht had proved his point but was unwilling to reveal his secret, although the smell of almonds emitted with the exhaust fumes indicated the presence of cyanide in the fuel. Enricht happily admitted that cyanide did make up a portion of the secret formula but refused to elucidate further until his lawyer was able to patent the secret. Strangely enough, emissions from motor vehicles have proven to contain a form of hydrogen cyanide, although this is unrelated to Enricht's secret formula. So, after his triumphant validation, Enricht's invention gained some serious interest, with piles of letters gathering on his doorstep while the telephone rang incessantly. The letters, like the phone, went unanswered. It was only after a gentleman by the name of Dr Thomas Freas refuted Enricht's claims that the old inventor felt galvanised to use his public voice once again. According to Dr Freas, Enricht's invention was impossible as he claimed: "There is no chemical that can be added to water that will make it combustible." Dr Freas went on to explain that, although water can be broken up by electrolysis, that process would require exactly the same amount as energy as that produced by burning, with the end result of absolutely nothing: "That is, nothing would be gained."

Enricht smiled mysteriously as journalists appeared on his doorstep to hear his defence of the green fuel. "What I'm about to tell you, Enricht explained, "is a simplification of a very complex development." Isn't that what everyone says when they want to sound clever but don't really have any answers? He went on to explain that the chemical he added to the water could separate the hydrogen atoms from the water and, upon their liberation; they combine with the oxygen atoms in the air and produce an explosion of power. He admitted that the reaction was both unlikely and unscientific but maintained that this was the process that had powered the car in his previous demonstration.

Fundamentally, Enricht was confronted with the same problem as his successors, Leach and Ahmad – those damned rules of thermodynamics! The first rule of thermodynamics declares that a system cannot produce more energy than that which has been put in; otherwise, we would all enjoy perpetual motors that never stop. As the amount of energy required to liberate the hydrogen atoms from water is equal to the amount of energy produced when those atoms ignite, the result is, as Dr Freas asserted, absolutely bugger all.

Anyway, back on Long Island in 1916, one reporter asked Enricht if he would be willing to lend his formula to the engineers of the Automobile Club of America. He said he would consider, adding that anyone in any doubt about his invention should speak to Ben Yoakum, a well-regarded financier who had previously held the role of president of the St. Louis and San Francisco Railway. Yoakum confirmed Enricht's claims and said he used the fuel in his own vehicle. With Yoakum's support came potential fame and fortune and all the big players in the automobile world wanted a piece of Enricht; in fact, Henry Ford wanted all of him and sent a representative to Long Island to retrieve the inventor and deliver him to Henry's office forthwith. Enricht was uncooperative, however, and, in the end, it was Ford who jumped on the train and journeyed to Enricht's home to make him an offer on his unique invention.

Mr Ford offered to purchase the rights to the secret formula provided it passed a series of rigorous tests which he would facilitate by providing a brand-new vehicle on which Enricht could continue his experiments. Of course, Enricht's claim that this alternative fuel would cost as little as 1c a gallon had serious repercussions for the motor vehicle industry and was one Henry Ford could not afford to overlook. Although this was the only investment Ford made into Enricht's invention, the inventor made the most of it and leaked a story to the press that Maxim Munitions Corporation Company had offered $1 million for the formula. It seems Enricht hoped this would encourage Ford to make an answering offer, but it had the opposite effect and Ford withdrew from the scene and threatened to sue Enricht should he fail to return the loaned car. Whether the Maxim offer was true or not is difficult to establish. According to some accounts, Hudson Maxim had asked, Dr Miller Hutchison, to attend Enricht's original demonstration and report back to him with his conclusion.

An inventor himself, Hudson Maxim started out working in his older brother's gun factory before establishing his own Maxim Munitions Corporation Company. Maxim was fascinated by explosives which is probably why he had such interest in Enricht's invention. In the end, however, the results of Dr Hutchison's own experiments were enough to cause Maxim to withdraw his offer if it had ever existed. After seeing the initial demonstration, Dr Hutchison was intrigued and returned to his laboratory to attempt to emulate the secret formula. Having taken a good whiff of the exhaust fumes, Hutchison had already figured out that the cyanide was only there to mask the smell of the other ingredients, which his well-trained nose had been able to identify anyway.

Once back in his laboratory Dr Hutchison discovered that it was possible to mix acetylene gas with acetone to stabilise it and to transform it into a liquid form which can then be dissolved in water. Dr Hutchison's experiments proved as successful as Enricht's and, the following day, he returned to the naval base where he had witnessed Enricht's demonstration and performed one of his own. The engine cranked and started just as it had for Enricht.

Surely this means a happy ending to the story of Enricht and his gasoline alternative? Sadly, it doesn't end here. Mr Smarty Pants, Dr Hutchison, noted that the water was nothing more than a vehicle to move the explosive acetone and acetylene solution into the cylinders. Furthermore, while Dr Hutchison confirmed that the solution was, in effect, a substitute for gasoline, the resulting damage to the engine was such that the fuel could never be effectively used without destroying the vehicle itself, thereby making it both expensive and dangerous. In fact, further evidence suggests the engine would have a potential lifespan of just hours rather than years. Another small issue that Hutchison overlooked was that the mixture of acetone and acetylene worked out more expensive than gasoline – this was Enricht's second big fib.

According to some, Hudson had his own doubts about the "green gasoline" he had supposedly offered to purchase from Enricht and declared that, while his company may have an option on the formula, he had no intention of buying the rights until the formula had been thoroughly investigated and proven. This contradicted the information the press had received from Enricht which indicated that the Maxim Co. investment was a done deal. Hudson Maxim shed further suspicion over Enricht and his claims when he declared: "I never saw any of this substitute for gasoline, and the reports that I myself examined it are absolutely false. Why I have not even met Enricht."

This last statement by Mr Maxim seems to confirm other reports that Enricht had just been playing with Ford and Maxim, using their interest to pique the curiosity of Ben Yoakum himself. Nearly eighteen months after Enricht's initial demonstration, the news emerged that Yoakum had agreed to fund Enricht's National Power Motor Company Inc.

Here we enter some uncharted waters where reports prove inconsistent. According to one report, after Yoakum's initial investment, Enricht gave him a sealed envelope inside which, he claimed, was the secret formula. The agreement was that Yoakum wouldn't open the envelope until full payment had been made and, if he did, it would constitute a breach of contract. However, Yoakum also got cold feet after rumours started abounding that Enricht was, in fact, a German spy and subsequently opened the envelope only to find it contained just a couple of fairly worthless bonds. Another report states that Yoakum became convinced that the ageing inventor was negotiating with the German government in an attempt to sell his secret formula to the enemy. As a result, Yoakum opened a legal case against Enricht and secured a court order that forced Enricht to open his safety deposit boxes and reveal his secret formula. The contents of the boxes are reported to be the same as those in the envelope – a few Liberty bonds that Enricht had bought with Yoakum's money but no sign of a secret formula.

The German connection was bound to come out at some stage, especially given the anti-German sentiments rolling around the world at this point in history. Although German-Americans had been accepted into US society for decades, the intensification of the European war dislodged them from their comfort zone as fear and paranoia took hold. The 1916 presidential campaign brought anti-German sentiments to the fore and both candidates, Woodrow Wilson and Charles Evans Hughes, declared that Americans of German descent or parentage were potentially disloyal to the Allied cause and to America itself. Former President Theodore Roosevelt was also very outspoken against Germans and Americans of German descent were under a constant burden of proof regarding their attitude toward the war and their level of patriotism.

As a result, it seems maybe Yoakum was simply looking for an alternative to the fact that he had been monumentally scammed. As a respected financier, Yoakum would have wanted to avoid the loss of face associated with investing in a crazy invention and, by suggesting Enricht was involved with the German government, he could clear his name with very little effort at all. As it stands, there is plenty in Enricht's background to suggest that he was a conman, but little to indicate that he was either a

German spy or a sympathiser. After Yoakum's attempts at having Enricht tried for treason, intrigued reporters began digging up some skeletons from Enricht's wardrobe and were soon airing his dirty laundry in the national press.

It seems that, since his emigration from Germany, in around the late 1890s to early 1900s, Enricht had been fleecing unenlightened Americans for decades. His first con took place in 1903 when he swindled a number of investors out of thousands of dollars which, he claimed, would be used to build a new 20-mile railroad connecting Cripple Creek to Canon City, Colorado. From there, Enricht headed for Tennessee where he tried selling deeds to a 45,000-hectare piece of land that he claimed to have inherited. His account of the facts was farfetched, to say the least, with Enricht claiming to be descended from Patrick Henry, the famous founding father who made the notorious speech, "give me liberty, or give me death!". Seems odd to say the least as Enricht had only arrived in the USA a few years earlier, but facts don't seem to have played a huge role in Enricht's life. After his Tennessee tryst, the inventor had become more experimental and sold a process for creating artificial stone to investors in Europe. Nor did his colourful career as a conman end with the revelations that followed his mystery green fuel. In fact, Enricht seemed to be inspired by his exposure and, in 1920, began publicising his new invention which, he declared, could distil gasoline from peat.

Despite his string of scams, some people were still listening to Enricht's claims, and they proved particularly irresistible to a few who happily handed over money to see Enricht complete his latest invention.

According to Enricht, he had created a machine that could extract naphtha from peat and then convert it into a fuel that could be used to run combustion engines. Some had their doubts, however, and the district attorney of Nassau County opened an investigation into Enricht's claims. After scrutinising Enricht's bank accounts, the district attorney discovered that invested monies had been squandered on Enricht's gambling habit rather than being used to advance science. The same Doubting Thomas then called for Enricht to prove his claims by demonstrating his machine in court. The presentation was a failure, but one Enricht blamed completely on the fact that the machine had been dismantled and then reassembled, thus causing havoc to its finely tuned mechanisms. He was denied a second chance by the judge who tried Enricht for grand larceny and subsequently convicted him, sentencing him to seven years in Sing Sing prison.

In his defence, at least Enricht's second invention was scientifically feasible, and even his original water-fuelled car gained momentum as technological advances made it more viable. Stanley Meyer is the most famous water car inventor with the 'water fuel cell' he created and successfully demonstrated. Unfortunately, Stanley was murdered in 1998, and his car and research equipment were promptly confiscated by the Federal Bureau of Investigation – something that fuels suspicion in itself. Are authorities and governments trying to prevent the development of a water-fuelled vehicle so as to maintain control and influence through the global oil market? Maybe old Enricht was really onto something… then, again, it's hard to believe that Enricht had any real conviction that his green solution would be the answer to fuel shortages given his history as a conman. Enricht doesn't immediately come across as the typical conman as there is little to indicate that he was either likeable or particularly conversational – two characteristics that most conmen have in common. Enricht was fairly successful in his scams, however, and certainly applied a few techniques that have been commonly used by con artists throughout history. One such tactic that stands out is the scarcity ploy. Conmen usually make themselves difficult to find or contact after making initial contact with an intended mark. Enricht definitely achieved this after his initial green fuel demonstration, withdrawing as he did from the world and from Mr Ford in particular. Usually, conmen use this technique to convince the mark that he isn't the right person to be involved in the scheme. Obviously, Enricht's approach was somewhat different as he was using the interest of both Henry Ford and Hudson Maxim to eventually capture the attention of Yoakum who, incidentally, was also a resident of Farmingdale, Long Island.

It does raise the question of why Enricht targeted Yoakum in this venture. Certainly, as a financier, he had both the money and the reputation for providing substantial backing for the scheme, and maybe Enricht knew him personally and believed he would be able to, effectively, take his money and run. Nonetheless, Enricht surely knew that, sooner or later, the flaws in his invention would be exposed. Yoakum also lied on Enricht's behalf when he told the press that he was running his own vehicle on the elusive green formula. It's almost inconceivable that Yoakum had a hand in the scam – he was an upstanding and admired citizen who had been a leading railroad executive, actually building the railroads he attested to, unlike his neighbour Enricht. The notion that Yoakum was an accomplice, or shill, to the old inventor's scam is tenuous, to say the least. Usually, such people are under the impression that they have something significant to gain from the swindle which, in Yoakum's case is uncertain. Of course, if the green gasoline had really worked, he would have stood to make a fortune from the invention, and maybe this is why he became involved. Yoakum was keenly interested in the issues surrounding agriculture in the US and was a strong advocate of a cooperative farming society in which the growing and marketing of crops and other farm products could be done in such a way as to reduce the distance between farmer and consumer. Theoretically, the green gasoline would have gone a long way to reducing farmers' costs of sales and therefore been a great boost to agriculture as a whole. However, Yoakum wasn't known for his flights of fancy and appeared a dedicated man with some political aspirations.

In comparison with other successful con men throughout history, Enricht lacks certain personality traits that would have assisted him in his hoaxes. There is little to indicate that Enricht had a likeable enough personality to engage others enough to be able to manipulate them. According to psychologist and writer Maria Konnikova, a successful deception is dependent on the swindler being able to use two forms of persuasion that appeal to different facets of human behaviour. When convincing a person to commit to something, there needs to be both push and pull; the push is the drive that encourages them to act, while the pull is removing the torpor that prevents them from taking the first step. The records that pertain to Enricht's scams reveal little of his personality but don't appear to point to a man with the charm and influence needed to hoodwink industry leaders like Henry Ford. Maybe, in his earlier days, his German ancestry had worked in Enricht's favour as, before the First World War, Americans had generally perceived German immigrants to be hard-working, prudent and benevolent, none of which, in retrospect, seem applicable to the inventor.

Exploring the traits of con artists further, the majority seek a certain affinity with their victims so will often search for a sociodemographic group that is akin to their own heritage and background. Mind you, to associate with German-Americans in New York in 1916 was possibly not a very sensible move given the suspicions of German involvement and espionage following the Black Tom explosion in New York in 1916. In conclusion, it would appear that Enricht was maybe less of a con man, despite the evidence to the contrary, and more of an unorthodox scientist with blind faith in his own capabilities. Pseudoscientists throughout history have had a desire to enlighten the misinformed world by communicating their truth to the ignorant masses. Pseudoscience is perceived as being primarily harmless, although, when taking into consideration the "evidence" used by Hitler, for example, to galvanise the German population against the Jews, some doubt does creep in. According to Philip Ball, a columnist for an international science journal, the theory that water is a fuel will never be silenced due to water's rather mythical status. Since being identified as one of the four classic elements by Aristotle, water has gone on to power water wheels for the Roman Empire as well as still being responsible for driving hydroelectric plants all over the world. Sadly, the moment thermodynamics comes in to play, it's all downhill, but pseudoscientists have a knack for avoiding thermodynamics – killjoy that it is.

So, there really is no way for water to be an element, a fuel, to burn, to combust or do anything more than the multitude of amazing things it already does. But Enricht will rest easily in his grave, knowing that his discoveries are still being rediscovered, talked about, covered by the press and celebrated by pseudoscientists all over the world. If you think there is an end in sight to the theory of a water-fuelled car, think again – this concept is here to stay, and there will always be a few out there, be they con men, madmen or pseudo scientists, who believe that Enricht was really onto something when he produced his first demonstration back in 1916.

# COUNT VICTOR LUSTIG

Arguably one of the most famous con men in history was the

dashing Count Victor Lustig, considered by many to be the Heavyweight

Champion of the Art of the Swindle. This character took the confidence

game to new heights - let's say about as high as the Eiffel Tower is tall.

More on this later.

Certainly, during his colourful career, many, many people would say

that they not only met the man but also knew him well. Many of his victims

would actually go as far as to describe him as a close, "dear friend" and "as

warm and sincere a human being as they ever knew." Yes, the Count

excelled at making people feel comfortable, close to him and valued. He

gave those he met a sense of confidence and compassion and made them

believe that he really cared about them and their feelings.

They were all wonderful suckers. What made The Count most special was that he excelled at lying.

He was born as Robert V. Miller to middle-class parents in 1890's Austria/Hungary and lived an unremarkable life until age 19, at which time he was slashed across the face by a jealous boyfriend and decided that perhaps he needed to reinvent himself as something more – something a little larger than life. He started telling new acquaintances that the long, ugly scar on his face was from a duel of honour, and thus the Count persona was born. After all – who doesn't want to imagine that dashing, romantic picture of a sword fight at dawn? Calling himself a Count was probably more practical than a Viscount, which would probably have just confused people.

He was a quick student of the quick buck and practised billiards, poker and bridge. And cheating. Lots and lots of cheating. A gambler's life had an immediate appeal, and he was naturally attracted to places where he could find rich, hedonistic marks– which meant the Trans-Atlantic ships that constantly chugged back and forth between Europe and New York. It was on trips like this that he met professional gamblers like Nicky Arnstein, and learned to polish his techniques for both legitimate and illegitimate play. Yes, it was a golden time to be a card shark.

The outbreak of World War One put a stop on the Count's adventures on the high seas, as the rich weren't all that attracted to being shot at or sunk while there was fighting going on and the cruise traffic dried up. However, in New York the Roaring Twenties were about to begin, there was a booming stock market, and everyone was doing The Charleston, ignoring Prohibition and getting rich, so Lustig packed up his tricks, charm and scar and relocated there. It was a classic case of "follow the money".

The year 1922 found him in Missouri, where he leveraged his charm, imagination and that wonderful scar of his to position himself as Austrian nobility, spinning elaborate tales of a lost family fortune due to the upheaval of the European war and a desire to rebuild through an honest get-back-to-the-land-through-farming yarn. This is the tale that he told the president of the 1st Bank of Missouri while expressing a keen interest in acquiring a dilapidated and barren farm there. The bank president had been trying to unload the farm since a recent foreclosure, and sensing that he might be able to make a bad loan good, wined and dined Lustig for weeks trying to close a deal. Eventually, the Count offered up $22,000 in Liberty Bonds for the purchase and persuaded the salivating bankers to also exchange another $10,000 of bonds for cash, to give him operating capital. They enthusiastically agreed to his terms and ponied up the money. However, they were so busy congratulating themselves on selling a worthless farm to this charming immigrant that they didn't notice Lustig switching the envelopes with the bonds and money, so that he made off with the bonds and their cash and blew town immediately, probably while the bankers were still chortling and toasting their success.

The bank immediately hired detectives to chase him down, and they finally caught up with him in a New York City hotel room. After being returned by train to Missouri, our hero the Count made a bold presentation to the bank's board of directors announcing that the worst thing that they could do was prosecute him – it would no doubt undermine public confidence in their institution and a run on the bank by all their depositors would surely follow. Evidently, he made a convincing argument, as they agreed to drop the charges and settle for a return of their money. However, not one to miss an opportunity for blackmail, Lustig went a little further and insisted that they pay him $1000 cash to compensate him for his inconvenience, noting that he had spilt some brandy on his silk smoking jacket when he was arrested. The bankers paid up, and the Count promptly jumped on the next train back to New York.

A short time later, Lustig leveraged two of the favourite traits he looked for in his dupes – greed and the thrill of betting on what looks like a sure thing. He invented the scam known as The Wire. If you've ever seen the movie The Sting, The Wire was the big scam that was the finale. The Count targeted a Vermont banker named Linus Merton, probably on the basis that anyone named "Linus" just had to be a born sucker. He had a pickpocket friend lift the man's wallet and cash only to have Lustig return it to him a short time later, instantly gaining the man's trust and confidence. A few friendly drinks with the grateful banker followed, during which he rolled out the Lost European Family Fortune Tale again. He told Merton that he had a cousin who was in a position to intercept horse race results a few crucial moments before they were announced to the gambling houses and bookmakers. This meant sure-fire horse race betting wins, and he "helped" his dupe to place a few low-level bets on races that had actually already been run. Naturally, the banker saw immediate results and the more he won, the more he wanted to bet. Who doesn't love winning a bet, especially with no risk? The fish was hooked. At just the right time, Lustig pulled the plug, announcing that his cousin was just about to quit, ending their winning streak. This put the pressure on for one more, grand slam bet that would make Merton's fortune – and of course, he bet the largest sum he could, and lost everything. The Count skipped town with $30,000 of poor Linus's money.

Next came probably the most famous con in history – the selling of the Eiffel Tower. While visiting Paris in 1925, Lustig happened in a newspaper article decrying the tower's condition. Originally built for the 1889 World's Fair thirty-six years earlier, the tower was never intended as a permanent structure and was considered by many snotty Parisians as an eyesore. The news article went on to say that the cost of refurbishment and repair was high and that there might be a move by the government to just tear the whole thing down and sell the metal for scrap. Reading this, Lustig was inspired and decided that, if anyone was going to make money from all that metal recycling, it was going to be Victor Lustig. The greatest scam in history was about to unfold.

First, he reached out to a confederate who just happened to be an expert counterfeiter and had official looking government stationary created, giving himself an official sounding title and credentials. Next, he sent vague letters to the five largest scrap metal dealers in the country, summoning them to a hotel room meeting to discuss "possible government contracts of significant value." Naturally, they all showed up, probably rubbing their hands in anticipation. After the customary wining and dining, Lustig made the grand announcement that the decision had been made by the government to tear down and scrap the tower and that the meeting had to be kept secret, as the move was controversial and discretion was essential. Although he invited all dealers to make bids on the project, he wasn't interested in the highest offer – he was only interested in identifying and fleecing the best mark for the scam. The lucky victim was André Poisson, which may have sounded a little fishy. André was new to the industry and anxious to make a name for himself. A suave dog that he was, the Count made sure to let it be known that he was open to a juicy bribe, which Poisson eagerly agreed to pay to cement the deal, eventually giving Lustig more than a million dollars in fees and bribes. A suitcase full of money in hand, Lustig skipped town and made his way to Austria with a pal, settling down for a few days to sip coffee, take in some sun and scan the Paris newspapers for news of the biggest scam in history. And then, nothing happened.

Interviewed later, he recalled that as the days and weeks went by he was more and more convinced that Poisson hadn't gone to the police or the press at all, probably out of embarrassment. As his idle time turned into months, he decided that there was no reason not to go back to Paris and simply do it again – and so he did.

On his return to Paris, he promptly sent out the same letters of introduction to the next five largest players on his list in France, inviting them to show up and be his next victims. Clearly, these leaders of industry didn't share much, as none of them had any inkling of what had happened with the first round of suckers and they all showed up, hoping to win a juicy government contract. Count Lustig probably couldn't believe his luck and proceeded to fleece another mark out of an even larger amount than he had the first. Unfortunately, this time when he fled back to Austria his victim wasn't as discreet as poor André Poisson – and the story broke in the papers shortly after he left the country. Victor had the good sense to pack up his money and head back to the United States, reportedly just hours ahead of his pursuers.

Safely back in America, the Count decided it was too much trouble and stress conning other people out of their money – he would just make his own and call it a day. Today this is called "counterfeiting". Actually, it was called the same thing back then but was a lot more sophisticated than loading up a photocopier and hitting a button.

1926 found Lustig back in New York, where he took an existing con called the Money Box and elevated it to a new level of perfection. Now history calls this scam "the Romanian Money Box" in honour of the Count. Never mind that he was actually Austro-Hungarian; Romanian sounds exotic enough. He was still working out how to print his own money, but thought until he perfected his ideas it would do just fine to convince other people that he could do it.

Lustig first contracted a cabinet maker he knew in New York to make him a number of well-crafted mahogany boxes, about 12 inches square, with a slot in either end to fit paper money and filled with very interesting wheels, gears, springs and whatever else he could think of to make it look "high-tech" in 1926 terms. The whole thing did nothing, but it did have a nice handle that turned the gears and some pretty knobs.

He then turned up in Palm Beach, Florida, where he convinced a well-heeled sucker named Loller that this was a one-of-a-kind money printing machine that actually produced legitimate money, so it was legal. He demonstrated by inserting a crisp $1000 bill into one slot in the machine, a piece of cotton paper in the other, and then turning the knobs and handle and lying his face off about what secret mechanical processes were happening in the machine while Loller watched. He explained that part of the process was an immersion of the blank cotton paper in a chemical bath, which would take precisely 6 hours, so he and Loller went off to dinner while they waited. Returning later, a few turns of the knobs and handle produced not one- but identical $1000 bills. The Count insisted that they head to the nearest bank to verify that the notes were genuine, which they were. Loller was impressed and promptly handed over more than $240,000 to buy the machine. He headed off home with his new money machine – Lustig made for the nearest train station and headed out of town.

Naturally, he had concealed two real $1000 bills in the machine, after carefully altering the serial numbers to match and therefore sell the illusion. The "6-hour chemical treatment" was nothing more than his guarantee that he would have at least 6 hours to get away before it was discovered that the machine didn't work. He really could have taken his time getting away from Loller, since it came out later that this unlucky victim kept trying to produce bills for weeks after parting with his money. One wonders how he explained to his wife why he needed to keep going out to buy more cotton paper.

The Count spent several months crossing the country after this, selling his money box for thousands of dollars, blowing town and planning his next move as a counterfeiter when he ended up at the wrong end of an arrest by a Sheriff in Oklahoma on non-related fraud charges. Sensing that the well-meaning lawman had a little larceny in his heart, Victor pulled out his one-of-a-kind box again, showed it off and offered up a bribe – the box in exchange for his freedom and $10,000 in cash. The Sheriff and the County Treasurer were both suckered in, and even bought our hero a new shiny suitcase to haul away his money in. They probably even drove him to the train station afterwards.

This case is particularly noteworthy because the Sheriff in question evidently wasn't keen on spending his golden years locked up amongst all those people he had spent arresting over the years – and vowed to track down The Count. Eight months later, he succeeded, and poor Victor opened the door in his Chicago hotel room to find a revolver pointed at his face. Master Con Artist that he was, he didn't panic and feigned ignorance and concern, eventually defusing the angry lawman by explaining that the whole thing was a misunderstanding and actually a result of not following his instructions to operate the machine properly. He offered up a perfect solution – he furnished the Sheriff with more details on turning the knobs and handle and provided him with a complete refund of $10,000. Completely satisfied and a little curious about making the bill-printing machine work, the Sheriff holstered his weapon, shook hands and departed, even using the new suitcase to carry the money. The Count was even more satisfied a few weeks later when he read a newspaper account of how the Sheriff was arrested on Bourbon Street passing phoney $100 bills and sentenced to Federal prison time in Pennsylvania. Victor was ready at last to begin a large-scale money printing operation.

By the mid-1930s, the authorities had noticed a virtual flood of counterfeit bills in circulation, all of high quality and popping up coast to coast. Eventually tracing the source, they were led to Count Victor Lustig and his network of forgers. Tracking down and arresting him proved difficult, and a special task force was formed after the sheer amount of phoney money began to give rise to fears that if it continued it might disrupt and undermine the national monetary system. Law enforcement started calling any fake bills "Lustig Money".

Eventually, of course, it all came to an end. In 1935 a jealous girlfriend turned him in, leading to his capture, arrest and what promised to be a sensational trial. One last hurrah followed when he escaped from prison the day before he was due to appear in court, but he was recaptured in Pittsburgh of all places. Sentenced to 20 years in Alcatraz, he died of pneumonia at the age of fifty-seven. His death certificate listed his occupation as a salesman; "con artist" has never been a recognised profession.

During his career, he fleeced people of hundreds of thousands of dollars, travelled the world and successfully "beat the rap" in more than 40 court cases where he was brought to trial for fraud. He will always be best known as the Man Who Sold the Eiffel Tower – twice.

# THE PONZI SCHEME

When thinking about swindlers and conmen, most of us will find

the name Bernie Madoff lurking somewhere in our memory banks. Pulling

off one of the biggest financial scams of recent history, Madoff has earned

his place in the history books, having run a huge swindle that continued for

decades and accumulated approximately $64 million. By comparison,

Ponzi's accomplishments are rather more humble, with a scam that lasted

little more than the year 1920 and accumulated around $20 million. Maybe,

in retrospect, the pyramid scheme scam should be renamed the Madoff

scheme? It is doubtful, however, that Madoff has the charisma that Ponzi

enjoyed. In fact, imagine for a moment, Madoff coming face to face with

the namesake of his scam, Mr Ponzi himself– would they be friends or

enemies?

Ponzi's autobiography, The Rise of Mr Ponzi: The Autobiography of

a Financial Genius presents a charming, witty man who was both

imaginative and opportunistic. Not the financial whizz that Madoff proved to be, Ponzi has been described as a "financial idiot" by his former publicity agent, William McMasters. Nevertheless, Ponzi managed to convince a vast swathe of Boston's population that he could, in the words of Boston Traveler journalist, Neal O'Hara, "turn decimal points into comas on almost any bank-book".

While Madoff had a glowing reputation as a successful financier, Ponzi had nothing to engender faith from his investors, and yet they happily threw money at him. Whatever his secret, I doubt this little flash man would have endeared himself to the micromanaging womaniser that Madoff is purported to have been. Himself quite adept at charming the ladies, I fear the two would have come to blows over both women and money.

An Italian by descent, Charles Ponzi was born to a family with aristocratic ancestry but little real money. While his mother ostentatiously retained the title of Dona, funds were limited, and Ponzi took on a job as a postal worker as soon as he was able. His commitment to gainful employment was fairly haphazard from the start, and he soon enrolled at the University of Rome, La Sapienza. His dedication to his studies matched his commitment to work, and his friends described his student years as an elongated "four-year vacation" in which he squandered his legally-gotten gains at various bars, cafes and visits to the opera.

With little to recommend him as either an academic or an employee, Ponzi's family encouraged him to emigrate to the United States where they assured him he couldn't help but make a fortune. In Ponzi's autobiography, he recalls them saying, "Go and make a fortune and then come back... as if amassing a fortune in America was something which could not be helped. In the United States, the streets are actually strewn with gold; all you have to do is stop and pick it up."

Inevitably, the reality of Ponzi's arrival in the US was at odds with his family's predictions, although he admits that his later scam meant that, "In fact... I didn't even have to stoop down to pick up the gold. In 1920 it was actually tossed into my lap; not by the pennyweight and with a teaspoon, but in large lumps and with a steam shovel." Nevertheless, Ponzi arrived in America financially bereft. Although he boarded with $200, by the time the ship docked on US soil Ponzi had gambled away everything bar his last remaining $2.50.

America didn't fling open its arms to welcome Italian immigrants in 1903 and Ponzi battled against poverty alongside his fellow countrymen. Initially, his lack of command over the English language worked against him but, once he had mastered the basics, he managed to secure a number of menial jobs, including the position of the dishwasher in a restaurant where his bedroom was the kitchen floor. Eventually fired even from this lowly position, purportedly for theft, Ponzi decided to head for Montreal where his newfound English language skills, as well as his ability to speak French, convinced Louis Zarossi to employ him as an assistant teller in his recently opened bank, Banco Zarossi. As its name indicates, the bank's customers were primarily Italian immigrants, making Ponzi a perfect candidate.

Banco Zarossi proved to be a solid training ground for Ponzi, and it was here that he was introduced to the concept of "Robbing Peter to pay Paul" – the name given to Ponzi schemes before the infamy of his own scheme made it his namesake. Although it appeared that Zarossi's bank was going from strength to strength as a result of the high-interest rates offered there, as Ponzi rose up through the ranks, the fragility of the bank's economic position soon became clear. Zarossi was suffering as a result of bad real estate loans and was reduced to covering his customers' interest payments from the money deposited in recently opened accounts. There was no profit at all.

The next chapter in Ponzi's tale is rather ambiguous. If you take Ponzi's word for it, an old school friend took advantage of Zarossi and convinced him to sign a forged cheque. In his autobiography, Ponzi claims he was already imprisoned at the St. Vincent-de-Paul Federal Penitentiary when this incident occurred, having been arrested and charged for forgery as a result of, once again, his enigmatic old school friend furnishing him with $200 for a business trip to some of the independent branches of Banco Zarossi. Other reports contend that Ponzi did, in fact, forge a cheque in the name of one of the bank's former customers, Canadian Warehousing.

Either way, Ponzi ended up serving three years in the penitentiary where conditions were far from comfortable. Despite having described himself as "a student and a man of frail physique... not cut out for manual labour," earlier in his autobiography, Ponzi then claims he excelled at crushing rock – the job assigned to the inmates at the penitentiary.

According to him, "... I figure I crushed enough rock to gravel the Yellowstone National Park. I got to be so proficient at it.... [that] [h]ad they kept me at it a little longer, I would have flattened that province down smoother than a pancake!"

Ponzi didn't remain crushing rocks for long, though, and once his "prowess received recognition", he was promoted repeatedly, culminating in a job as the warden's clerk. According to Ponzi, this was the highest position available to inmates: "I couldn't go any further up without stepping out of the gate." In 1911, Ponzi was released from prison –liberty which he claims resulted from him being pardoned. In his words, the warden warmly patted him on the back and said, with "fatherly inflexion", "You have deserved it, Charlie." And thus the "dapper little Italian" was free to go and go he did – almost straight to another prison.

Again, Ponzi claims that the criminal act that saw him incarcerated for the second time was a completely innocent act on his part. Having been released from prison, Ponzi found himself penniless once again and was dependent on friends to give him a roof over his head. Another mysterious old school friend comes to the rescue and suggests he heads back to the US where his prison record would be unknown. The same friend loans Ponzi the money for the fare and then asks him to accompany five of his friends who are travelling in the same direction. Newly arrived from Italy, the friends were wide-eyed and tongue-tied, and Ponzi would be doing his friend a great service if he just escorted them on the train and ensured they alight at Norwood.

A US immigration officer arrested all six men as soon as the train entered the US on the basis that they had violated the immigration laws. Despite Ponzi's protests, he was imprisoned alongside his newfound friends for a further two years. This period of detention added another feather to Ponzi's cap after he befriended Wall Street businessman, Charles Morse. According to Ponzi, "Charlie Morse was a pretty good sort of fellow. Loaded with money. Liberal. A good mixer. And extremely well versed in Wall Street finance. He could read the stock exchange quotations backwards." He was also something of a conman in his own right and soon secured his release from prison through malingering. By eating soap and "other stuff", Morse managed to convince the prison doctors that he was suffering from "locomotor ataxia or of Bright's disease". His seemingly hopeless condition meant his life was in danger, and he was subsequently pardoned by President Taft after serving just over two years of his 15-year sentence. Ponzi is clearly amused by this, commenting that, "Once released; naturally he declined to die. He must've lived another dozen years or so."

Ponzi had to wait a little longer for his own liberation and, when it came, he headed west. He claims this was a terrible mistake and some years later, astrologers would inform him that his "stars pointed to the East". With the benefit of hindsight, Ponzi claims the astrologers – whoever they were – were right; after all, "To become enlightened, a man ought to travel always in the direction of the sun. Every yap knows that." With some of his charisma shining through, Ponzi wittily admits that heading east isn't always the easiest option, "the eastern routes are so crowded with blue lodge members [members of the Freemasons] that a traveller must sit up all night to get to a railroad ticket-window ahead of them."

By a rather convoluted journey, Ponzi ends up in a small mining town where many Italians have made their home. Eking out a living acting as interpreter, occasional small-time bookkeeper and male nurse, Ponzi hits on the idea that the mining camp needs both light and running water. He says, "To decide with me is to act. Even in those days, I was no slouch at promoting. For a very good reason, that money with me is always the last consideration instead of being the first. Why should I worry about money? Money is always around to be had. The main thing is to have an idea. A plausible idea which can be dressed up and sold."

Unfortunately, Ponzi's efforts were thwarted after an accident in the kitchen of the company hospital resulted in one of the nurses sustaining severe burns. While Ponzi wasn't close to the victim, Pearl Gossett, he performed a heroic act which led Mitchell Zuckoff to later describe him as, "Clever and charismatic, at various times he was a hero -- saving the life of a young nurse by literally giving her the skin off his back -- and a criminal...".

Ponzi says, "It did not seem fair that a young girl like Pearl should be permitted to die such a horrible death. That nurse had been so kind to her patients that it seemed inconceivable that she should meet with such ingratitude. It made my blood sizzle to think that any person could be so selfish, so cowardly as to refuse a mere inch of his own skin to save a human life."

And so, he stepped up to the challenge and agreed to a series of rather horrifyingly primitive skin grafts that would see him donate a huge section of skin from his back and legs and leave him languishing in a hospital for nearly three months. The operations resulted in saving both Pearl's life and her arm, and, for Ponzi, a few complications such as pneumonia and pleurisy, "Economically, it just blew my power plant to smithereens! But again, I may say: What's a power plant more or less in the land of Insull? A trifle! A mere trifle! He did not miss it! And neither did I. Not much."

Soon after this incident, Ponzi headed to Boston in search of employment and, instead, found love, in the form of Rose Maria Gnecco. It was love at first sight for Ponzi, but Rose's family were less than convinced. Although Ponzi kept his criminal record secret from his sweetheart, Rose's mother uncovered the truth and exposed him to her daughter. It was too late, however, and the young couple married in 1918 and Ponzi embarked on another series of jobs, including working for his father-in-law's grocery store. He had little success, however, and the family's fruit stall was soon flailing in financial uncertainty.

The following year, Ponzi decided that "If I was an asset to any employer, I was a greater asset to myself." Having failed to prove his worth as an employee, this is a rather bold move but, as he admits, he soldiered on anyway, "Never figuring that I might be one of those assets which are spelt without the final 'et'." Setting himself up in a rather dingy office in Boston's School Street, Ponzi embarked on a business in which he attempted to sell his money-spinning ideas to people he knew back in Europe. His success was far from immediate, and he tried everything he could think of to generate an income but with little success. "I looked for money everywhere. Found it nowhere. Nevertheless, I kept up the struggle to the end. Pawned the family jewels. Mortgaged the household furniture. I didn't sell my soul to the devil because he found he could get it for nothing if he waited long enough for it."

The IRC (international reply coupon) fraud that he subsequently embarked on "actually fell in my lap like a ripe apple. I did not have to shake the tree to get it. I just reached over, where it had fallen, and took it. It looked good. Luscious. I examined it for flaws. Found none. I had to bite. I wouldn't have been human if I didn't."

In a letter from a company in Spain enquiring about Ponzi's advertising catalogue, Ponzi found an international reply coupon which had been sent to enable him to send a swift response at no cost to himself. IRCs enabled the recipient to send a letter to a correspondent in another country and were priced at the postage cost of the country of origin. After the First World War, inflation had made a serious dent in the cost of postage in Italy, meaning that an IRC originating in Italy could be exchanged for US postage stamps worth considerably more than the original IRC. Ponzi figured he could make a return of around 400% using this form of arbitrage. Even better, the scheme was completely above board. "There was no law or rule or regulation I could possibly violate by trafficking in coupons... The most that could be said was that such traffic might have been unethical. But a breach of ethics was not an infraction of the law. Anyway, the environment had made me rather callous on the subject of ethics. Then, as now, nobody gave a rap for ethics."

With no real credit to his name and no way to prove himself as a serious trader, Ponzi's attempts at securing a bank loan were met with derision so. Instead, he set up a stock company and, with the trust and investments of his friends, set to work. The first month saw him bring in enough to get him off the ground and, as he paid what he promised to his first few investors – double their money in 90 days – so he went from strength to strength. "People gambled with me as I thought they would. They gave me ten dollars as a lark. When they received fifteen at the end of 45 days, all sense of caution left them. They plunged in for all they were worth."

As the scheme gained momentum, largely thanks to an ambitious salesman employed by Ponzi, so he set up his own company. The Securities Exchange Company was established in January 1920 and grew feverishly, with income growing from $5,00 to $25,000 in just two months! By July, Ponzi was raking in nearly $1m a day. Despite the tsunami-style cash flow, the company was actually running at a huge loss. The only way Ponzi had to pay his investors was from the money of new investors. Although some reports indicate that Ponzi merely surfed the wave, giving little thought as to how he could generate genuine profits, he claims that he was feverishly trying to buy IRCs to achieve his original vision. The problem was, quite simply, supply and quantity. While he could have, potentially, secured the 53,000 postal coupons required to pay the arbitrage profits to his first 18 investors, by the time 15,000 venture capitalists were committed, he would have needed a fleet of ships to transport the necessary IRCs from Europe to the US. It was an untenable position.

Nevertheless, the snowball had started rolling and showed no sign of stopping. While his first flush of investors were mainly immigrants like himself, investing a little here and there, as the news spread, more lucrative investors were drawn to the flame. At the peak of his success, almost 75% of Boston's police force was committed to the scheme, along with members of the upper echelons, bankers and many more besides. "People must have thought I had discovered the buried treasure of the Incas. Or Aladdin's lamp. If they gave a thought at all to the coupons, they must have got dizzy figuring how many of them I needed to justify what I was doing. In fact, my visible resources back then were more than $5,000,000. Assuming I earned two cents on each coupon, I should have had to handle over 250,000,000 of them! It was absurd. There were not that many in the world. There had never been that many. And it would have taken months to print them!"

Certainly, once the press got hold of Ponzi's success, they were a little bemused but conversely eager to support the little man. According to the Rochester Times-Union, "...whether the Ponzi bubble bursts or not, the American people will take off their hats to a fellow so clever as he." The Washing Evening Star concurred, saying, "whether he retires a millionaire or is finally detected as a swindler, Ponzi must stand as a remarkable figure."

The truth was that while outwardly going from strength to strength, Ponzi was in a pickle. He had been unable to secure any IRCs at all for some months. The unusual activity in the IRC department had led to a suspension of the sale of coupons in a number of countries. Even if he had been able to buy, he certainly couldn't meet the promises he had made to his investors. Ponzi was stuck between a rock and a hard place, faced with the choice of owning up and facing prosecution or keeping on with the scam and hoping for the best. Looking back, he says, "It never occurred to me to pocket all the ready cash and duck out. If I had, I wouldn't have been called the darn fool as many times as I have been.".

Although fully aware of how precarious his position was, Ponzi kept up the swindle and maintained all the trappings that attested to his financial ascension. Driving to and from his new offices in the latest Locomobile, Ponzi set himself and his wife up in a Lexington mansion and then brought his mother over from Italy in first-class style on board an ocean liner. For his mother, however, America was not paved with gold, and she died shortly after her arrival. Ponzi continued throwing money around, donating $100,000 to an Italian Children's Home in his mother's honour and purchasing various companies and shares to produce legitimate profits that could be used to pay his investors.

With thousands of investors, and money being bandied around as though he were printing it himself, it's no wonder others within the financial sphere began to query his meteoric rise to wealth. Every time a negative article appeared in one of the local papers, Ponzi would quickly reassure his investors and pay out those who wanted to flee. This worked effectively, and many of those seeking to withdraw their investments subsequently reinvested them on the strength of Ponzi's prompt pay-outs. Investigations continued, however, and the Boston Post put a couple of their best investigative reporters on his tail while the Commonwealth of Massachusetts were also busy digging into his paperwork. In such situations, Ponzi would make the first move, using his charm and quick mind to divert attention away from his haphazard bookkeeping.

Nevertheless, he could only keep people looking the other way for so long, and when the Boston Post contacted a financial journalist, Clarence Barron, Ponzi's precarious position began to falter. Barron's first observation was that Ponzi himself had not invested in his own scheme – a fact that raised doubts immediately. Barron then discovered that the number of postal reply coupons required to keep Ponzi's scheme afloat far exceeded the actual number in circulation. Furthermore, the overheads of purchasing, redeeming and transporting the coupons would have made serious inroads into the profit. Barron went on to conclude that, even if the system was legitimate, it was far from ethical. To do what Ponzi claimed he was doing, he would be profiting at the expense of either a foreign government or the American government itself, making the scheme both unscrupulous and immoral.

This was the beginning of the end for Ponzi, although he fought hard, canvassing his investors and passing out free coffee and doughnuts in an effort to secure their continued support. Despite his efforts, over a period of three days, he paid out $2m, drawing the attention of the United States Attorney for the District of Massachusetts. Attorney Daniel

Gallagher then secured the services of Edwin Pride to audit the Securities Exchange Company – a task that proved formidable even to the most experienced auditor. The sum total of Ponzi's bookkeeping was a series of index cards with investors' names on.

To curb the increasingly negative image of his company and himself, Ponzi hired a publicity agent to create a more positive impression. Sadly, Ponzi picked the wrong man when he employed William McMasters, and this error was to contribute significantly to the collapse of his scheme. Unimpressed with Ponzi's talk of coupons, McMasters became highly suspicious of his employer and subsequently revealed some incriminating documents. Rather than creating positive publicity for Ponzi, McMasters sold his story to the Boston Post for $5,000, with the resulting article putting one of the first nails in Ponzi's coffin.

By this point, the sums of money involved in Ponzi's scheme were substantial enough that, if the whole thing collapsed, it threatened to take Boston's entire banking system with it. At this point, the Bank Commissioner for Massachusetts became involved and, noting the large loans Ponzi was taking out from the Hanover Trust – a bank he had invested in heavily and had a large, controlling share in – Commissioner Joseph Allen concluded that things weren't quite as rosy as Ponzi would like everyone to believe. On discovering how overdrawn Ponzi was on his Hanover Trust account, Allen put a stop on the account and approached some Ponzi's smaller investors, encouraging them to file for involuntary bankruptcy. Armed with unfavourable information, Allen then approached some Ponzi's investors to come forward to assist with the investigation.

Ponzi's "house of cards" was collapsing and Pride's audit gave it a hefty shove, revealing Ponzi to be $7m in debt! With news of his previous arrests dominating the front pages alongside his involvement in Zarossi's disgraced financial enterprise, Ponzi was, in his own words, "licked." Knowing the federal authorities were straining at the leash to arrest him, Ponzi had little choice and turned himself in. As Ponzi reflects in his autobiography, "My house of cards had collapsed! The bubble had busted! I had lost! Lost everything! Millions of dollars. Credit. Happiness. And even my liberty! Everything, except my courage."

Ponzi faced 86 charges of mail fraud and was sentenced to five years in prison. In addition to the collapse of the Hanover Trust, a further five banks folded, and his investors lost a total of around $20m, receiving less than 30 cents for each of the dollars they had invested. After serving three and half years of his sentence, Ponzi was released, only to be indicted on state charges of larceny. Ponzi hadn't been expecting this, having assumed that these charges would be dropped in recognition of his co-operation and having pleaded guilty to the federal charges. Without missing a beat, Ponzi sued for double jeopardy – a case that made its way steadily up the ladder of jurisdiction, before being ruled against him in the Supreme Court.

Ponzi found himself in court once again, this time answering to a number of larceny charges. Without a penny to his name, Ponzi was forced to represent himself in court and called upon his charm and powers of persuasion to sway the jury in his favour. Winning his first trial, Ponzi appeared again to answer the remaining five charges against him. The jury was deadlocked, leading to a third trial in which he was, finally, found guilty and sentenced as "a common and notorious thief" to seven to nine years in prison. Ponzi recognised, "Unquestionably, I was licked. For the time being. But no man is ever licked unless he wants to be. And I didn't intend to stay licked.".

True to his word, as soon as he was released, Ponzi headed for greener pastures and set up the Charpon Land Syndicate in Jacksonville, Florida. His new enterprise offered to sell sections of land, promising investors a 200% return within 60 days. The "land" he was selling was swampland, and most of it was still underwater, but this didn't deter the ambitious Italian, well, not until he was indicted by the Duval County grand jury and sentenced to another year in prison. After an appeal and a $1,500 bond, Ponzi fled, attempting to board a merchant ship bound for his homeland. However, he was quickly captured and sent back to serve a further seven years in a Massachusetts prison.

On his eventual release, Ponzi was deported, leaving his beloved wife Rose behind while he attempted to find a legitimate job and create a new home for her in Italy. After two long years of waiting, Rose gave up on her husband and, in 1937, divorced him and attempted to leave the rumours behind her by heading to Florida, where fewer people knew the infamous name, Ponzi.

For the remainder of his life, Ponzi continued to hop from one scheme to another, with little success. He eventually secured a job in Brazil with the Italian state airline but lost it again when the airline's operation was shut down as a result of the Second World War. Ponzi's health subsequently went from bad to worse, with a heart attack leaving him enfeebled and encroaching blindness limiting his capabilities. After a brain haemorrhage left him partially paralysed, it wasn't long before he drew his last breath, passing away a pauper at a charity hospital in Rio de Janeiro on 15th January 1949.

Regardless of Ponzi's success or otherwise, his scheme and charisma left its mark on the world and his name on the future of scams and of pyramid schemes in particular. In the last interview he ever gave, Ponzi said of the American people, "Even if they never got anything for it, it was cheap at that price. Without malice aforethought, I had given them the best show that was ever staged in their territory since the landing of the Pilgrims! It was easily worth fifteen million bucks to watch me put the thing over."

Ponzi's notoriety is partly to do with circumstance and timing. According to author Mitchell Zuckoff, "We remember Ponzi because he had this amazing combination of charisma and great success... it was this moment in 1920 where money became king and newspapers were all over it. He hit that sweet spot of money and media that elevated him and made his name indelible."

While Madoff's scheme has been labelled "elegant yet evil", Ponzi's has been declared as "far-fetched" but fundamentally different in that Ponzi's was based on a legitimate concept, even if that source could never grow to fruition. As a "dapper little man with the straw hat, the walking stick and the boutonniere," Ponzi somehow wormed his way into the hearts of the American public, with his fans calling him "the greatest Italian of them all." By comparison, I doubt that anyone will be calling Madoff "the greatest American of them all" at any point in history.

# MIDDLE EAST COMMAND CAMOUFLAGE DIRECTORATE

It's one thing to pull a rabbit from a hat and quite another to make 107 miles of canal disappear, but if anyone could do it, it would surely be someone from a magical dynasty, like Jasper Maskelyne. A stage magician like his father and grandfather before him, Maskelyne seems a somewhat unlikely wartime hero, and yet he has been credited with some of the world's greatest deceptions including hiding the Suez Canal and creating a decoy replica of the harbour at Alexandria. A great magician who helped to win the Second World War or an egotistical conman with an inflated sense of his own importance? The Maskelyne name is well-respected in the world of magic and in his book, The Great Illusionists, Edwin Dawes describes the Maskelyne family as "a dynasty that has no parallel in the annals of British conjuring and ... cannot be matched anywhere in the world."

According to Jasper Maskelyne's own accounts of his life and work, he believed that his skills as both a magician and a camoufleur far surpassed most other men, although his son, Alistair, insists that most of his father's success and acclaim resulted from his lineage rather than his own talents. Alistair Maskelyne is quoted as saying, "... I recall being quite incredulous, as a small boy, that he should get so much financial respect from British firms acquainted only with his family reputation, and not with his real situation..."

While little is documented about Jasper's early life, he came from a pretty magical family, with both his grandfather, John Nevil, and father, Nevil, being stage magicians. It seems Jasper's life was already planned out for him when he entered the world on 29th September 1892. Up until the early 1930s, Jasper performed alongside his brothers, Clive, Jack and Noel, at their London base, St George's Hall. Relations between the siblings became strained, eventually leading to Jasper being dismissed from the magic Maskelynes in January 1933. Although given permission to continue performing, the termination agreement meant that he couldn't take any of the equipment or perform under the name of Maskelynes Ltd. The company, however, didn't survive long after Jasper's departure and went into receivership two years later.

Jasper himself was certainly not having an easy time of it, and his son recalls there was often not enough money to pay the bill for groceries at the end of each month, especially not once he had invested in materials to create some of the onstage machinery necessary for his illusions. As a result, Jasper was keen to find new sources of income and, in 1936, wrote the Book of Magic which revealed various tricks Jasper had kept up his sleeve, so to speak. This kept the family in the black for a short while but then, when Jasper was later approached by a mysterious ghost writer who was keen to write a history of the magical family, he eagerly agreed.

The book, White Magic: the story of Maskelynes opens with the question, "What is magic?" and the first chapter concentrates on how the art of illusion first came into the lives of a family born to farm. Jasper (or rather, his ghostwriter) recalls that, while his grandfather had little aptitude when it came to agriculture, he had a love of mechanics, "For his tricks were almost all of them beautiful demonstrations of applied mechanics." Apparently, John Nevil was not only the foremost magician of his era but also invented the pay toilet. Perhaps not something Jasper wished to draw too much attention to!

The rest, in effect, is history and we would be deluding ourselves if we were to continue reading White Magic in the hope that it would reveal any truth. According to Jasper's son, Alistair, there is little in the book "related to truth, because the ghostwriter had happily invented whole sequences outside of the essential history. My father seemed not to mind these fictitious events." Mind you, what would expect from an illusionist? Jasper's accounts from his 1930 tour of South Africa are particularly adventurous, with stories of curses from a Zulu witch-doctor and how he helped to heal a girl with a "poltergeist quality" by recommending a change of scene and air for six months. It would seem Jasper was not one to play down his achievements!

White Magic was the forerunner to the subsequent Magic: Top Secret written by the same mystery ghost-writer and published in 1949. While Maskelyne may not have had a great deal of input into the book, it certainly adheres to what his son says when he describes his father as being "most self-creative in his own imaging. All of his geese were swans." Jasper's son goes on to recall how he took his father to task over the amount of "over-dramatised fiction" in this supposedly factual account. He claims to have suggested that the book be rewritten to give a sense of Jasper's achievements as a serving officer. Alistair's suggestions were promptly dismissed by the ghost-writer, saying, "there were thousands such. It would never sell."

Some years later, author David Fisher relied heavily on the information contained in Magic: Top Secret to write his own book on Maskelyne, entitled The War Magician. Although Fisher also borrowed some of Jasper's diaries to gain additional material for his narrative, he never met Maskelyne so gained much of his insight from Fisher's original text. According to Alistair Maskelyne, Fisher's book is, as a result, "much a work of fiction." The diaries lent to Fisher, and oddly never returned, primarily comprised newspaper cuttings and photographs with little text. Although arranged chronologically, the diaries contain very little information and Fisher's subsequent manuscript is, in Alistair Maskelyne's opinion, "only 40% reliable: all the personal relationships and much of the sequences are fictional."

It appears this information hasn't yet been leaked to the general public and any search on the worldwide web will leave you pretty convinced that certain events detailed first in Magic: Top Secret and subsequently in The War Magician really did occur. Some military historians reiterate these proceedings with the type of serious hyperbole that makes them hard to doubt. As Roland Barthes asserts, "Myth is invulnerable to mere facts".

Much of what is written about Maskelyne concerns his wartime efforts. Maskelyne attempted to enlist in the army as soon as war broke out, although his first applications were ignored. Maskelyne eventually joined the Royal Engineers in October 1940 and was subsequently trained in the area most relevant to his on-stage talents – camouflage. While some were sceptical about his assertions, Maskelyne joined many others in training at the Camouflage Development and Training Centre in Farnham in the south of England. While Maskelyne claims to have found the training rather boring, given his prestigious abilities at hiding things on stage, others say he had a little flair for the job. According to a fellow trainee, Julian Trevelyan, Maskelyne was fun to have around and great for an evening's entertainment but "rather unsuccessful" when it came to actually camouflaging items that would prove advantageous to the war effort.

According to some reports, Maskelyne was nonetheless determined to prove himself and took the opportunity to further his soldiering calling by proving his capabilities to a certain Inspector General. Maskelyne prepared for the forthcoming inspection by disguising a machine gun bunker. Apparently, his camouflage was so perfect that the General literally walked into the gun. The account of this incident appears in Magic: Top Secret and the way it is written sounds like something out of a children's adventure story! Maskelyne sounds young, naïve and extremely arrogant.

In this version of events, it is the highly respected and decorated John Standish Surtees Prendergast Vereker, Sixth Viscount Gort that Maskelyne amazes with his abilities, as he should have! According to Maskelyne's account, "I got to work on that machine-gun post with everything short of Black Magic; and my men were as excited as I was to make a job of it." On their arrival in the field to view the bunker, the visiting group look around in bewilderment, unable to see the bunker at all. When someone suggested that, maybe, the orders had changed, and the bunker was in the next field along, the group began to retreat. Holt, however, called out, "Halt!" as he was standing, looking into the barrel of a machine gun. Sounds a bit like the Famous Five with uniforms, doesn't it?

It was this incident that spearheaded Maskleyne's army career for all intents and purposes, and Maskelyne was signed up by Brigadier Dudley Clarke and sent to Cairo to work for M19, the department responsible for infiltrating resistance networks in Europe and using them to help get stranded airmen back to Britain. Maskelyne's duties involved the development of concealed devices similar to those created by the formidable Q in the James Bond movies. From there, Maskelyne headed to the camouflage unit based not far from Cairo and was briefly in charge of the Camouflage Experimental Section established in November 1941. The brevity of his command is indicative of his success – lasting less than four months – after which he was "transferred to welfare" which is a nice way of saying they got rid of him, stopped him from doing anything remotely important and assigned him the duty of keeping more effective soldiers entertained with magic tricks.

The official version of this story is that Maskelyne created an elite team after conducting rigorous interviews with over 400 candidates. The 'Magic Gang' that developed had all the aspects of any good soldering unit – a cartoonist, a carpenter, a chemist and some electrical engineers! While it is claimed that Winston Churchill praised the work of Maskelyne and his gang, former British soldier, Richard Stokes, argues that no such gang ever existed. This is endorsed by author Rick Stroud who penned The Phantom Army of Alamein and describes Maskelyne's memoirs as "fantasy". Stroud points out that Maskelyne was transferred long before many of the events he claimed to be involved in even occurred.

Nevertheless, even the official MI5 website pays tribute to Maskelyne's positive involvement and influence during the war, crediting him with masterminding a significant ruse at the de Havilland Mosquito factory situated to the north of London. The "attack" was designed to convince Germans that a bomb had exploded in the factory and create the illusion of extensive damage to the factory. While the deception is true, the matter of Jasper's involvement is a little harder to believe. Maskelyne was in Egypt at the time of the hoax, and his name is notably absent from the declassified documents which describe the event.

One of the most famous and retold stories of Maskelyne's great illusions was touched on earlier in this article and involves the disappearance of the Suez Canal. An extraordinary feat were it true! Certainly, some evidence indicates that the canal was invisible – how else did the Germans fail to close it down? The canal was vital in terms of the Allied strategy, and there is little explanation as to how it was defended or how it managed to remain usable throughout the war. According to Maskelyne's account, he and his Magic Gang, having learnt some useful techniques while making the harbour of Alexandria disappear, vanished the canal with systems of lights and mirrors. We'll get back to Alexandria shortly but let's just take a moment to visualise a canal adorned with "dazzle lights".

According to Maskelyne, he and his Magic Gang were requested to come up with a plan that would protect the Suez Canal from German bombs. As an important supply line, the canal was vital to the Allies' war effort but couldn't be covered with canvas – a project too vast and expensive to even consider! Instead, Maskelyne came up with the idea of creating a barrage of light that would distract and confuse the enemy. He supposedly created a Whirling Spray of spinning light beams using 24 anti-aircraft searchlights and mirrors to construct a rotating arrangement of light and reflection. According to Maskelyne, this is the sole reason the Suez Canal remained open and operational throughout the war, unimpeded by the Germans. As photographs of this wall of light are published in Magic: Top Secret, there can be no denying that the Whirling Spray camouflage was built. The question is: was it ever used?

In an attempt to reconstruct some of the more inventive approaches employed during the war, the BBC aired a programme in which this whirling spray of light was recreated in miniature to demonstrate its efficacy. Crafty Tricks of War transmitted the episode in 2004, with the reflective cone central to the construct being powered by a rubber band and a narrow sheet of plastic representing the canal. The demonstration was far from convincing and served only to prove that moths are easier to fool than Messerschmitt aircraft.

There is no evidence to support the notion that Maskelyne's Whirling Spray was ever actually put into action, although it is known that a prototype was built, and even declassified intelligence reports make no mention of it. The British press, however, remains faithful to the idea and to Maskelyne's legacy. The London Times ran an article in 2005 about The Magic Circle's forthcoming celebrations in which they describe Maskelyne as, "The Magician Who Hid a City. He performed some of his greatest illusions in Egypt... [including] concealing the Suez Canal using spinning strobe lights."

In his 2008 article on the use of strobe lights, David Hambling discusses the Canal Defence Light which was a searchlight that could be mounted onto a tank and used to illuminate the battlefield as the tank advanced. The lights were fitted with a shutter that enabled them to flicker six times a second. This created an effect similar to strobe lights at discos and clubs and was so strong it could temporarily blind the enemy, improving the attackers' advantage. Hambling quotes a Major-General JFC Fuller, who is acknowledged as a key figure in the development of armoured war in the Twenties, as saying the failure to use this weapon was "the greatest blunder of the whole war".

So, Maskelyne wasn't the only person contemplating the use of lights to cause confusion and disorientation and to debilitate the enemy's sight.

He was, however, the only one with a grandiose enough view of himself to claim his inventions were key to winning the war. As Hastings asserts, "A very colourful account of Maskelyne's role is given in the book The War Magician - reading it, you might think he won the war single-handed".

The story of how the harbour of Alexandria was saved from night-time bombing has been declared "the greatest camo story ever told", and it is, indeed, impressive. The intention was to create a decoy which would draw the enemy's bombs away from the true harbour, leaving it intact and operational. Apparently, hundreds of men were involved in creating the dummy harbour which was situated at Maryut Bay. Maryut is situated approximately 9km from the harbour of Alexandria, so this is viable as a decoy location. However, the geographical references and description of the location of the decoy harbour are inconsistent with any real topographical facts about Alexandria and the surrounding area.

Maskelyne supposed masterminded the creation of everything, if the account in Magic: Top Secret is to be believed, from "dummy men, dummy steel helmets, dummy guns by the ten thousand, dummy tanks, dummy shell flashes by the million, dummy aircraft..." By then turning off all the lights at Alexandria and turning on those in Maryut Bay, the Luftwaffe pilots were drawn to bomb the wrong location. This meant that the entire light grid and lighthouse had to be recreated at Maryut Bay, along with fake explosions and a mock counter attack. As soon as the bombers departed, Maskelyne and his crew would hurriedly litter the area with paper maché rubble to convince the reconnaissance pilots cruising over during the day that the attack has been a success.

There is much written about this deception, and it is widely believed that the illusion was so successful that similar techniques were used to disguise other important naval bases, although cynics claim that the entire idea is rather ludicrous, as is the notion that Maskelyne masterminded it.

According to *The Times*, the "grandest of grand illusions" took place the day before the battle of El Alamein in October 1942. Again, this deception ran along the lines of creating a decoy army in a different location to confuse the Germans and was coupled with Operation Canwell which sent out false information via radio.

The previously fired Maskelyne was recalled to assist with the production of the so-called sun shields. These were hinged canopies that fitted over a tank to mimic the appearance of a truck, thereby disguising the tanks. The operation is widely considered a success, a point that Stokes concedes, while still adamantly refusing to acknowledge that Maskelyne played any part in the deception. According to Stokes's take on the Alamein scenario, it was thanks to the RAF that the position of the Eighth Army remained hidden from the Germans. Stokes notes that "the enemy was denied any aerial observation of the British forces between 18 and 22 October... and during 23 October, immediately before the Eighth Army's advance..." Decrypted information from Enigma, the German's code, supports this claim.

Geoffrey Barkas, who was in charge of the Middle East Command Camouflage Directorate, humbly admits that the battle was not won "by conjuring tricks with sticks, string and canvas... [But] it was good to feel that camouflage had helped to put the fighting men into battle on more favourable terms..."

Of course, there were many unsung heroes working behind the scenes during the war, many of whom died before documentation attesting to their contributions was declassified. Take Alan Turing, for example. Persecuted for most of his life because of his homosexuality, Turing is believed to have killed himself in 1954 after being "chemically castrated". Turing was arrested and found guilty of gross indecency in 1952 and given a choice between imprisonment or hormonal treatment to reduce libido. He opted for the latter.

Before his arrest, Alan Turing had worked in top secret at Bletchley Park, creating the machine that broke the Enigma code and enabled the Allied forces to gain some serious ground. It is believed that the war was shortened by at least two years thanks to the work of Turing and his fellow codebreakers. This curtailment saved the lives of an estimated 14 million people. Turing was given a posthumous royal pardon in 2013.

Like Maskelyne, Turing died in obscurity, with his war efforts unacknowledged and his achievements silenced due to the need for absolute confidentiality. Stories such as Turing's add some weight to Maskelyne's heroic legacy. If Turing's technological breakthroughs went unsung for so many years, surely another hero whose strength was illusion could also have been kept under wraps for the same reasons? However, even though many documents have now been declassified and new information made available, there is nothing to corroborate Maskelyne's claims – no photographs, no documentation and no eye-witness accounts.

Part of the problem could be that the Magic Gang didn't exist and people that don't exist have a tough time producing evidence to prove, well, anything at all. Of the key members of Maskelyne's Magic Gang, Michael Hill was supposedly a private whose main talent was getting hold of certain items and materials that were nearly impossible to procure. According to all the records I could find, there is only one Michael Hill who was enlisted in the army during the Second World War, and he was enrolled with the Hawaiian Department. The role of this department was, as its name suggests, the protection of Hawaii. Wonder how he made it to Egypt, then?

Next up is Theodore Graham, nicknamed 'Nails', due to his brilliance with hammer and nails. There are a few more Theodore Grahams in the archives, but most of them enlisted only after Maskelyne's Magic Gang had already been disbanded. The character, Bill Robson, is fleshed out a little more in Maskelyne's book and, while there were a fair few William Robson's enlisted, none of them were cartoonists. There was a radio presenter and a naval officer, but that's about it. According to Richard Stokes, Maskelyne created the character of Bill Robson, using real-life Punch cartoonist, Brian Robb, as his inspiration. This is corroborated by other documents that attest to Robb's presence in Alamein.

Sergeant Jack Fuller was purportedly Maskelyne's right-hand man, a disciplinarian with an in-depth knowledge of the area. This character did actually exist and is buried at the Alamein Memorial in Egypt. The only problem here is that he died in 1941, a whole year before the Alamein deception and just a few months after Maskelyne's arrival in Egypt. Another key member of the Magic Gang was a Phillip Townsend, who is described as a homosexual artist. There was a very famous artist by the same name, but he only came into existence some years after the war. During the Second World War, a Phillip Townsend flew with the RAF and was equerry to both King George VI and Queen Elizabeth II. It wasn't him that flirted with the non-existent Michael Hill, then? He was too busy conducting a romance with Princess Margaret! As for identifying the last gang member, one would have to have Sherlock Holmes's powers of detection to achieve that! The only thing recorded about Mr T was that he was black.

Author Peter Forbes sums up Maskleyne's part in the war quite succinctly, saying his role was "…either absolutely central (if you believe his account and that of his biographer) or very marginal (if you believe the official records and more recent research)." Other sources suggest that Maskelyne was encouraged to take credit for some ideas, including the sunshield tank disguise, to encourage the Allied High Command to support such techniques while keeping other key personnel undisclosed. Maybe Maskelyne came to believe this rhetoric or maybe his over-inflated sense of his own abilities was already in existence prior to his enlistment.

In an extract from Magic: Top Secret, Maskelyne ghost-writes that, during the training he received in camouflage techniques, he could have "hidden me and most of the rest of the class so efficiently that the lecturers would never have found them in the duration of the war". Certainly, a rather over-inflated ego coming to fore there! Similarly, science writer Phillip Ball's 2014 book, Invisible: The Dangerous Allure of the Unseen describes Maskelyne as being entirely unsuited to military life, suggesting that the army regretted their decision to use wizardry and camouflage once they realised that "their war wizard was an incorrigible egotist and fantasist".

On the other hand, according to an article written earlier this year by Akarsh Mehrotra, the documents about Maskelyne's wartime exploits will only be declassified in 2046, leaving his greatest tricks unacknowledged during his lifetime. "The magician, just like his illusions, disappeared in the pages of history." One only has to search the name, Jasper Maskelyne, on the internet to know this is far from the truth – there is endless material both supporting his claims and querying them. There is little written about Maskelyne after the war, although it seems he did return to the stage and continued with his travelling magic show. It's not clear whether Maskelyne was driven to drink by the death of his wife, Evelyn, in 1947 or because of the lack of official recognition for his key role during the war, but it certainly impacted on his career. His son, Alistair, remarks that "During this period the travelling show gradually moved to firstly the second layer or level of music hall circuits, and later, still further to the third level, in small towns like Minehead..."

Maskelyne later left Britain with his new wife, Mary, and headed for Kenya where he either became a police officer or a driving instructor, depending on which report you read. It will be interesting to see if the movie, The War Magician, which has been in the pipeline since 2003, ever does get made and, if so, what angle the director will take. Similarly, I personally can't wait for 2046 to feast my eyes on the declassified documents that will finally prove whether Maskelyne's role in the war was as important as he claims, or whether his greatest hoax has been convincing the Great British public of his own importance. If the latter is true, then Richard Stokes will have hit the nail on the head, "Jasper Maskelyne's most effective piece of camouflage, his most deceptive decoy, was ... built from recycled tree carcass and weighed only 13 ounces. It was a hardback book called Magic – Top Secret."

# CATCH ME IF YOU CAN

Running away from home at the age of 16 is not uncommon in today's society. However, while most runaways find themselves ill-equipped to fend for themselves in the cut-throat world we live in, one, in particular, found a way, not only to feed and clothe himself, but also to see the world and become one of the most notorious imposters in American history, while pocketing around $2.5 million. The story of Frank Abagnale is known to many, thanks to its success as both a box-office hit and a musical, but what does this really tell us about Frank? Was he a genius conman or just a lost, confused child with little concept of the consequences of his actions?

Frank William Abagnale Jr. was one of four children born to Paulette and Frank Abagnale Sr. In an interview on Talks at Google, Frank describes his father as a Daddy – one of the highest accolades he could give. A Daddy is someone truly involved in the upbringing of his children, whereas a father is just the man who provided the biological impulse – at least, I think that's what he was getting at. Frank portrays his father as a loving influence – a man who never once missed kissing his children goodnight and telling them how much he loved them, even when they were teenagers standing over 6ft tall! Frank, however, abandoned his family and went adrift, surfing his way through a series of roles and alter-egos as he sped his way around the globe and up the social ladder of success. What possessed him to leave his family and set out on a white-water journey of lies and deceit?

Although both the movie and other documents available on the internet indicate that Abagnale's parents separated before him running away from home, his own version is much more compelling. According to Frank, he was pulled out of school at the tender age of 16 and driven to a courthouse where he was told his parents were waiting for him. Arriving in the courtroom, he stood in front of the judge and, for the first time, heard of his parents' intention to divorce. Due to his age, Abagnale was instructed to decide which of his parents he would prefer to live with. It doesn't take a wild imagination to envisage the stress and anguish this caused for the young boy. Rather than answering, Frank bolted for the door, tears streaming down his face. He was never to speak to his father again and remained estranged from his mother for many years.

According to Helen Deutsch, a psychologist, many imposters start off in life being raised in successful homes, just like Frank, whose father was a successful businessman and a respected member of the Rotary Club. In keeping with the imposter's psychological profile, Frank's sense that he was entitled to a life of success and social status was denied once the IRS started investigating his father for tax fraud and his parents' marriage began to fall apart. Resentful and embittered, Frank had no opportunity to begin climbing the ladder of success – he was too young to get a foot past the first rung – so, instead, he grabbed at a status that he hadn't earned but could easily steal. In his own words, Abagnale states, "A man's alter ego is nothing more than his favourite image of himself." So, this is what he projected to the world and what the world, foolishly, accepted as the truth.

Of course, Frank didn't simply walk out of the courtroom and into the cockpit – his first move was to grab his chequebook and a few other possessions and head for New York. Having worked for his father's stationery store as a delivery boy, Frank went in search of similar jobs. While he quickly secured such a position, the pay was commensurate with his age and wouldn't go far in terms of keeping himself fed, clothed and with a roof over his head. Frank had his chequebook to hand, however, and when money got particularly tight, he would cash a cheque for a few dollars, dipping into the savings he had accumulated during his brief working life.

The situation wasn't sustainable, however, and Frank realised that a change of tack would be required if he was to keep his head above water. With height on his side and a mature appearance that denied his youth, his fellow students had often remarked that he looked more like a teacher than a pupil. Inspired by this thought, Frank carefully adjusted the date on his driving license, adding 10 years to his age. When he next went in search of work, he found he was offered improved wages, if nothing else. But this still wasn't enough.

As Frank explains in his Google Talks interview, there was nothing premeditated about his cons; they were purely based on opportunism and youthful confidence. Nonetheless, it's mind-boggling to think that a 16-year-old boy managed to pull off this next stunt. On seeing an Eastern Airline crew coming out of a prominent hotel in New York, Frank's mind started clicking through a number of associations. Pilots and others in uniform were treated with a deference that is both unthinking and, for the most part, unconscious. If Frank could secure a uniform, he could also secure a more commanding presence that inspired trust and confidence. A friend of his had remarked that he could easily walk into a bank and cash a cheque. Frank agreed but asserted that his cheques were good so there would be no reason for them not to be cashed... and then he clicked – if he walked with confidence, oozed a little charm and wore a fancy-looking uniform, the world could, realistically, be his oyster.

In pursuit of this new goal, Frank's mind started working a lot quicker than most of ours ever do and he promptly phoned the Pan Am International Airline head office to explain that he was a pilot on a fast turnaround, having arrived in New York early that morning and due to fly out again the same afternoon. Unfortunately, the hotel's laundry service left much to be desired and, as it stood, he had no uniform to wear for his return flight. The office promptly directed him to the closest outlet stocking their uniforms, and off he went.

Once measured up and suitably attired, Frank inquired whether he should pay in cash. The attendant responded saying they didn't take cash. Cheque, then? Nope. Just sign for it, and the company will deduct it from your next paycheque. Easier than taking sweets from young children! But a uniform alone would not be enough. Every member of the airline's crew, from the ground crew to air hostesses to pilots, all carried a plastic ID badge. Being plastic, it couldn't be changed or written on, so Frank turned his attention to the Yellow Pages and browsed through until he found companies that produced such items. Within a few phone calls, he had located the very firm that made ID badges for Pan Am. Feigning to be the procurer at a company who was blown away by Pan Am's system, he asked if he could pay them a visit to check out the equipment and see some samples.

Dressed to impress in a civilian suit, Frank headed off and arrived at the appointed company to be greeted warmly – after all, they were about to do mutually beneficial business together. On asking to see a sample, the person assisting him hurried off and returned with a large laminated sheet of paper on which was a copy of an ID with SAMPLE written across it in large letters. This was no use to Frank, but as he, in his guise as a buyer, was looking to buy the whole system, he asked to see it in action – using himself as the Guinea pig. A short while later, he walked out with a near-perfect ID card – there was just one thing missing – the Pan Am logo. Popping into a nearby toy shop, Frank located a small toy aeroplane which carried the Pan Am insignia. Carefully, he removed the decal from the plane and fitted it snugly into the top corner of his ID card, sealing it back together with, presumably, glue as well as a little cunning. He was all set to embark on a con that would keep him going for several years, give him access to over 26 different countries and tuck a mammoth one million air miles under his authentic pilot belt.

Obviously, it wasn't all plane sailing (sorry – couldn't resist the pun!). Although dressed to kill in his pilot's uniform, ID badge at the ready, Frank headed to the closest airport, La Guardia, where he wandered around looking for inspiration as to how best to capitalise on his new look. Taking a seat in the staff canteen, Frank was soon joined by a few pilots from a rival company. Frank realised his inexperience and naivety when he was asked what equipment he flew. Frank puzzled about this for a second or two – surely this would mean the equipment in the cockpit? The controls? Which are electric, so he responded, "General Electrics". An upsurge of raised eyebrows greeted his response. "So, you fly a sewing machine, do you?" This was the beginning of a steep learning curve into the jargon pilots, and flight attendants use across the globe. His canteen companions went on to inquire what he was doing at LaGuardia, given that Pan Am only ever flew into JFK. Frank bid a hasty retreat and never did forget that his "equipment", so to speak, was the actual aeroplane, rather than the intricacies of its electronics.

Once at JFK, Abagnale was initiated into the art of deadheading, a term used by pilots when they secure a free lift on a passenger flight because, as an employee of another airline, they are on their way to complete a task elsewhere. Once he discovered that he could fly for free, book into hotels on the company account and even cash fraudulent pay cheques at either the hotel or airport, Abagnale discovered a life of freedom. Or did he? In Steven Spielberg's 2002 Movie, Catch Me If You Can, Abagnale is portrayed as a young man with much bravado and an aspiration to be the James Bond of the skies. While Abagnale's self-confidence is undeniable, in his own version of events he was far from the sharp-suited strutting figure presented in the film, although he did have a fondness for good clothing. He was still devastated by the collapse of his family and remains vehemently against divorce even in his 60s. Abagnale claims that most nights during his stint as an imposter at Pan Am, he cried himself to sleep. No one knew who he really was and no one he loved knew where he was. A lonely life, even if full of the things many of us desire – travel, money, luxury hotels and the freedom to be anyone you choose to be.

One of the most important lessons Abagnale's story teaches us is, quite simply, not to be too stupid nor too trusting. One of his most ridiculous scams was when he noticed that airlines and car rental companies would drop their daily takings into a secure drop box within the airport compound. Disguised as a security guard, Abagnale, posted a sign on the box stating, "Out of Service. Place deposits with the security guard on duty." Blindingly trusting, this is exactly what the car rental and airline representatives did, never stopping for a moment to consider just how a box could be out of order!

While Abagnale's pilot performance earned him considerable kudos, not to mention a fair amount of money and free travel to 26 different countries in just two years, it wasn't the only job he fraudulently applied for and secured. With the FBI on his tail, Abagnale knew his luck was running out, so he hopped off a flight in New Orleans, narrowly dodging arrest, and settled in Georgia for nearly a year. In securing the rental of an apartment, Abagnale decided against listing pilot as his profession for fear that the landlord may check up with Pan Am and, instead, declared himself to be a doctor. He subsequently befriended a real doctor living in the same apartment block and secured himself a position as a supervisor on the night shift, overseeing the work of the resident interns. Fortunately for both Abagnale and the hospital's patients, the position required him to do little more than organise and supervise, with the interns performing the real nitty-gritty. Although Abagnale may have sold his soul, his moral judgement was still intact so, when he realised that lives could be lost because of his ignorance – a young child nearly died as a result of Abagnale's lack of understanding when a nurse reported a "blue baby" – he quickly resigned from the position.

From the cockpit to the surgery and then from the surgery to the courtroom – Abagnale was nothing if not resourceful. One might expect that having secured cheque forgery as a way of making money, he may just rest on his laurels and enjoy the ride, but it seems Frank had other aspirations. By the time he was 19, Abagnale was still posing as Robert Black, a first officer for Pan Am, while simultaneously forging a law transcript from Harvard University, passing the Louisiana bar exam and securing himself a position as the State Attorney General's office. If only all 19-year-olds were as ambitious and persistent!

However, it's a bit of a blow to the egos of lawyers all over the world when Abagnale claims that posing as a lawyer was the easiest to fake. "I found most of it was a matter of research... and then basically persuading people that you're right and they're wrong...". Doesn't sound like you need to study for aeons to achieve that, does it? Clearly, Abagnale was unusually gifted – creative, intelligent and with the ability to think about problems until they seemed to disappear. The biggest problem of all, however, was how to exist as someone you're not without any support system for five long years from the age of 16.

So, was he a sociopath or just a lost kid in search of an identity? The imposter phenomenon is an interesting one and, as with many psychological diagnoses, it's hard to differentiate imposterism on a low-key scale from the simple desire to fit in and to please those around us. Are we imposters when we agree with someone just to keep the peace? Are we lying when we say everything is fine or are we just adhering to social expectations? The imposter phenomenon fascinates because, on the one hand, we fear being taken in by fakes and, on the other, because we fear our own personality is a sham. If you think back to being a child, you are encouraged to indulge in games of pretence and make-believe while also being encouraged to tell the truth. It's no wonder it can get a little muddled, especially for someone like Abagnale, whose sense of self was intricately woven in with his sense of family. Once the family unit disintegrated, so did his identity.

Strangely enough, the imposter is part of who we are as people. The word "person" came through the strange linguistic equivalent of an arduous donkey trek through ancient Italy, starting out as phersu which meant "mask". Perhaps being an imposter is a necessity in the socially complex world we live in or perhaps it's a fundamental part of being human. According to one of Shakespeare's more verbose characters, Jacques in As You Like It, "*All the world's a stage*, and *all* the men and women merely players; They have their exits and their entrances, and one man in his time plays many parts". We are not the same people as teenagers as we were when we were children and, as we become professional adults in a world of money and employment, we change even more. We pretend to ourselves and to others, retelling our stories in the context of different social circumstances. Similarly, many characters in Shakespeare's plays pretended to be someone else. Look at Viola pretended to be a eunuch in Twelfth Night or Rosalind who disguises herself as a shepherd in As You Like It. So, we all shift and change according to different circumstances. Some of us feel like imposters, even though our position has been earned.

According to Psychology professor Matthew Hornsey, "Impostors fascinate us, not because we want to be like them, but because deep down we worry that we are like them." Our insecurities lead us to doubt whether we belong in that director's chair or holding that scalpel in the emergency room. You fear you're just not as good and not as clever as your colleagues. Although Abagnale exuded confidence in his various guises, maybe on a deeper level he doubted himself. Perhaps blamed himself for the collapse of his parents' marriage. But if he could convince people he was a pilot, they would treat him differently and boost his ego and prestige, and the reality of who he really was would become negligible.

Imposters, like most con artists, prey on specific victim types. They look for those who appear lonely or are undergoing a significant change in their lives. Ironically, it is often a sense of loneliness or isolation, or a recent significant event, that motivates the imposter. As Abagnale admitted in a blog interview with SXSW, "...it was very lonely, I gave up my teen years... You could never make friends because people don't like to be deceived."

Nevertheless, Abagnale continued to run. He knew the FBI was after him, but he wouldn't surrender. Why? In Spielberg's film, the answer resounds with a cartoonist cat-and-mouse scenario – as long as the cat keeps chasing, the mouse keeps running. This seems to be pretty close to the truth and Abagnale admits, "...what started out as survival became more and more of a game. I was an opportunist, so when I saw an opening I asked myself, "Could I get away with that?" Then there was the satisfaction of actually getting away with it. The more I got away with, the more of a game it became - a game I knew I would ultimately lose, but a game I was going to have fun playing until I did."

Abagnale was eventually arrested in France in 1969, after being recognised by an ex-girlfriend working on Air France. The conditions of his year-long imprisonment in France were horrific – he was kept naked and alone in a tiny cell without any mattress or toilet facilities. This aspect of Abagnale's life is scrupulously recreated in Spielberg's movie. Although 12 different countries sought his extradition, he remained at Perpignon prison for a year before being extradited to Sweden where conditions were considerably more humane. Shortly afterwards, he was deported back to the US where he was sentenced to 12 years in federal prison for a long list of forgery charges.

Abagnale hardly rolled over and died once caught, however, and there has been much supposition about his alleged escapes from various authoritative hands – including FBI agent Joseph Shea who pursued Abagnale for several years. In the film, Catch Me If You Can, Abagnale manages to escape Shea's custody on the flight back to the US by squeezing through the hatch around the aeroplane's public toilet. The airline declares this an impossibility and Abagnale backs this up. Nevertheless, he maintains he did escape while the aeroplane was taxiing, sneaking out through the service area and making a risky run for it. But, given Abagnale's past, are we really sure this is the truth?

In another curious scene in the movie, Carl Hanratty (the movie version of Shea) enters Abagnale's apartment to arrest him but, before he can do so, Abagnale convinces him that he is not the criminal but, rather, a member of the secret service. According to Abagnale, this really did happen – it wasn't premeditated, it just occurred to him at that moment, so he tried it on to see if he could get away with it. If there are two things Abagnale has in spades, it's balls and brains!

Today, Abagnale continues in a similar line of work, merely exchanging the role of the mouse for that of the cat. Abagnale's role with the FBI started in 1974, while he was still serving his 12-year sentence. According to Abagnale, it was Shea who felt he could assist the FBI with fraud cases and tracking down con-artists and who helped secure his parole. In addition to working with the FBI, Abagnale formed his own company which advises on security issues and designs fraud prevention programmes. Abagnale is quick to assert that he is not proud of his imposter past, preferring to focus on the 37 years he has lived as a law-abiding citizen. In his mind, his greatest achievement is being a daddy, and he attributes his life on the right side of the law to his wife. This makes complete sense – finding a woman who would love him and give him a family gave him a new identity, a real one that brought both status and security, the two things he had been searching for during his imposter years.

Although three presidents have offered Abagnale a pardon in recognition of his subsequent work for the FBI, Abagnale has refused all of them. He prefers to live with the reality of his past now that he's in a secure enough place to reject the lies that motivated his criminal acts. While some of the events in his life may seem rather far-fetched, many of them are true, although he admits the author of his semi-autobiography, Catch Me If You Can, took a fair amount of poetic license in his summation of Frank's life, "I was interviewed by the co-writer only about four times. I believe he did a great job of telling the story, but he also over-dramatised and exaggerated some of the stories. That was his style and what the editor wanted.".

While in some ways Abagnale fits the psychological profile of an imposter perfectly, in others he is quite unique. Looking at his actions in the context of other famous imposters makes him considerably more likeable. Known as "the Great Imposter", Ferdinand Demara, lacked Abagnale's integrity and operated on numerous patients while impersonating a trauma surgeon during the Korean War. By comparison, Abagnale's impersonations are rather mild, and he carefully avoided having anything to do with the real work of a doctor during his tenure at the hospital and quickly resigned when he realised people's lives could be at stake. Nevertheless, Demara managed to save several lives, and none of his patients died as a result of his ministrations. Brilliance or luck? To be fair, a large part was brilliance – like Abagnale, Demara possessed a superior intelligence which was coupled with a photographic memory. Before attending to his patients, he quickly read and memorised a medical textbook and then set to work with the information he had absorbed.

Abagnale never claimed to be a genius and avoided performing roles that he wasn't qualified for; when handed the controls of an aeroplane, he promptly put it into auto-pilot, "... because I couldn't fly a kite." Despite throwing himself into a world of deception and lies, Abagnale maintained some sense of his own capabilities and the morality of what he was doing, limiting the damage he caused to others. "I don't believe I was a genius. I was an adolescent. I was just a young kid who ended up on the streets of New York."

In a sense, imposters and con men are dependent on one thing – our ability to con ourselves. According to psychologist and writer, Maria Konnikova, we are the true charlatans – those of us who are taken in and duped by the Abagnales out there. We believe we are superior to the people who would naturally be conned, and, with that sense of self-importance and self-aggrandisement, we believe that, because we believe, it must be true. She calls this our "inattentional blindness" which comes to the fore once we are invested in the conman's story and makes it nearly impossible for us to see the warning signs that litter the wake of the conman.

So, while Abagnale may be on the brink of being a sociopath, or just a fumbling teenager in the adult world, his confidence and quick-thinking could take him only so far – the rest was up to people just like you and me. Those who think we are above the norm, intellectually unable to be conned, confident enough to identify a fraud, smart enough to avoid a scam. In her book, The Confidence Game: The Psychology of the Con and Why We Fall for It Every Time, Maria Konnikova addresses the reader directly, predicting that most of us will "remain convinced that you, personally, have already properly taken [all these factors] into consideration." In other words, the majority of us assume ourselves to be superior to others and therefore above being scammed. With that perspective, it becomes clear that we are scamming ourselves.

So, to all those pilots, air stewardesses, doctors and lawyers out there, let go of your ego and be careful who you give your jump seat to, take caution before handing over the scalpel and think twice before appointing that smart young man as your next prosecuting attorney!

# THE HITLER DIARIES

When the editors-in-chief of the German weekly news magazine
Stern were offered the chance to publish the lost diaries of Adolf Hitler, a
kind of collective madness broke out. Convinced they had stumbled on the
scoop not only of the century but of all time, they allowed their hearts to
rule their heads. Common sense and journalistic caution were swept aside
by the prospect of soaring sales. Seasoned journalists, salivating at the
thought of making a name for themselves, ignored clear warning signs that
they were being sold a pup.

It was 1983, and while Hitler long been a hot topic throughout the
world, in West Germany interest in the cruel dictator was at an all-time
high. The airing of the American TV series Holocaust was forcing the
German people to re-evaluate their past and to try to come to terms with
their complicity in some of the worst crimes in human history.

There was a collective desire to understand the man who had presided over countless acts of barbarity, caused the death of millions and brought about the downfall of their country. Access to Hitler's diaries would offer an insight into the workings of the madman's mind and perhaps enable the German people to lay the blame for their shameful past on him and him alone. Little wonder then that the Stern editors fell hook, line and sinker for such an obvious hoax.

Felix Schmidt first heard about the Hitler diaries on the 13th of May 1981, the day Pope John Paul II was shot and wounded by a would-be assassin in Rome. One of Stern's three editors-in-chief, it was his job to ensure that the magazine capitalised on the story as much as possible. To this end, he asked his secretary to get hold of Gert Heidemann and have him in his office within half an hour. It was a tall order.

Heidemann, who worked in the magazine's contemporary history section, took his role as an investigative journalist very seriously and was rarely in the newspaper's offices, let alone at his desk. As it turned out, before Schmidt's secretary could locate Heidemann, Schmidt and his two fellow editors-in-chief – Rolf Gilhausen and Peter Koch – were called into the office of the magazine's publisher and given the news that thanks to the efforts of the elusive Heidemann, the magazine had gotten hold of the diaries of none other than Adolf Hitler.

Throughout subsequent meetings, Heidemann told the story of how the diaries had supposedly fallen into his hands. It all began, according to

Heidemann, on 20th April 1945 when the Third Reich was in its final death throes. On that day, ten planes flew from Gatow airfield under the command of Hitler's personal pilot. These planes formed the centre of Operation Seraglio, Hitler's plan to have his right-hand men and favoured party members removed from the Führerbunker in Berlin and flown to a command centre in southern Germany.

The final plane in the fleet carried ten chests of Hitler's personal items guarded by Sergeant Wilhelm Arndt who had acted as Hitler's valet. For reasons unknown, it crashed into the Heidenholz Forest some miles short of its destination. Precisely what was on board remains a mystery, although Hitler did say that his favoured servant Arndt had been "entrusted with extremely valuable documents which would show posterity the truth of my actions!".

This was tantalising enough to keep journalists and writers throughout the world hoping and wondering. According to journalist Robert Harris it also created "the perfect scenario for forgery." That a plane carrying items belonging to the Fuhrer had crashed in the Heidenholz Forest was well-known to historians, so the possibility of valuable documents being secretly recovered and kept hidden until now was a plausible one.

According to Heidemann, a group of farmers found the Hitler diaries and passed them on to a high-ranking East German army officer who now wished to sell them with Heidemann acting as his go-between. Heidemann went on to describe how the books were thrown from a moving vehicle into his car on a transit road in East Germany. In turn, Heidemann tossed over money to pay for the books in a similar manner. This part of the story failed to impress those gathered and was later adjusted, with Heidemann claiming the notebooks were smuggled into West Germany on a truck transporting pianos.

When Heidemann was asked to reveal the identity of the East German officer, he declined because doing so would put the man in danger. The editors grudgingly agreed on the need for the source to remain anonymous, and Heidemann was given permission to continue purchasing the collection, which he claimed ran to a total of twenty-seven notebooks. Meanwhile, efforts which lasted nearly two years were instigated to authenticate the diaries.

Handwriting experts in New York and Bern confirmed that the books were, in fact, written by Hitler himself. Schmidt, the editor-in-chief who has revealed the most about this episode, said a kind of euphoria had taken over at the Stern offices and even the most obvious indications that the diaries were forged were somehow ignored. It subsequently came to light that the handwriting samples supplied by Heidemann to compare the diary to were actually faked by the very same man who was busily creating the diaries.

Once the diaries were exposed as forgeries, things started to fall apart in the Stern offices. People urgently wanted to know how such experienced journalists, editors and publishers could have been drawn in by a clumsy forgery. It was then that the man behind the diaries was revealed to be a petty criminal scratching out a living in the unforgiving economic atmosphere of East Germany.

Konrad Kujau was born to Nazi supporters in 1938 near Dresden. As a born and bred Nazi, Kujau idolised Hitler long after the Fuhrer's suicide and the defeat of Germany.

Working at various unskilled jobs, Kujau first found himself on the wrong side of the law in 1957 when a warrant for his arrest was issued following the theft of a microphone from the Löbau Youth Club. Kujau fled to Stuttgart where he immersed himself in a life of temporary employment and petty crime. With his girlfriend Edith Lieblang, he opened a dance bar. When the bar failed and left him in financial difficulties, he embarked upon a career of counterfeiting and forgery. In this, as in many other things, he was not a success, and he was arrested and sentenced to five days in prison for the counterfeiting of 27 Deutsche Marks' worth of luncheon vouchers. Five years later, a routine check of his accommodation revealed that Peter Fischer, as Kujau was calling himself, didn't exist and Kujau was imprisoned again – this time for living under an assumed identity.

In the Seventies, a visit to his family in East Germany opened Kujau's eyes to a new and potentially lucrative source of ill-gotten gains when he discovered that many people in the area collected Nazi memorabilia. While it was illegal to trade or export these items, Kujau decided that the potential gains far outweighed the risks, especially as increased demand in Stuttgart was inflating prices to over 10 times the amount he needed to pay in East Germany.

As Kujau became increasingly interested and involved in the trade of Nazi memorabilia, his circle of collectors grew, which led him in 1974 to rent a shop where he could display his own collection and meet with fellow enthusiasts. Realising that a helmet from the First World War worth only a few marks could increase in value by several orders of magnitude if accompanied by a note stating it had been worn by Hitler himself, Kujau built a highly profitable business.

Much of that business involved the sale of documents supposedly handwritten by notorious Nazi leaders such as Rudolf Hess, Joseph Goebbels, Heinrich Himmler and Herman Göring, not to mention Adolf Hitler himself. Although he'd mastered the handwriting of these gentlemen, the rest of his work was pretty shoddy, with frequent spelling mistakes and grammatical errors. Worst still, it was all produced on modern stationery.

Later in the Seventies, Kujau branched out into art and started fabricating paintings which he attributed to Hitler, who had been an enthusiastic amateur artist in his earlier years. The subjects of his Hitler artwork were in keeping with what was popular among Kujau's friends and fellow collectors and, as a result, were far from the subjects that may have interested Hitler. One of his forged artworks even depicted a naked Eva Braun.

Nevertheless, this new branch of forgery proved successful and lucrative, encouraging Kujau to expand production to include poems supposedly written by Hitler, which he later admitted were so crude that "a fourteen-year-old collector would have recognised it as a forgery."

While hardly a master counterfeiter, Kujau was knowledgeable enough and had sufficient connections to appear a well-educated collector and trader of Nazi memorabilia. This led to him making the acquaintance of Fritz Stiefel, a wealthy collector from Stuttgart.

Kujau created a hand-written manuscript of Mein Kampf for Stiefel before moving on to producing an introduction to what he claimed was the undiscovered third volume of the infamous work. According to Stiefel, Kujau loaned him the first of Hitler's diaries in 1975, although Kujau contests this, claiming it wasn't until 1978 that he began work on the diaries. As luck would have it, Heidemann's fascination with the Nazis brought the journalist into the same circles as Stiefel, opening up for Kujau the opportunity to sell his fakes to Stern for a lot of money.

Heidemann himself was in urgent need of funds, having gotten himself into financial hot water by mortgaging his flat in Hamburg to purchase the Carin II, a yacht that had belonged to prominent Nazi Herman Goring. As a result of this purchase, Heidemann was catapulted into a world populated by former Nazis, including SS generals, and their offspring. To discover more about the yacht that was bankrupting him, Heidemann arranged an interview with Goring's daughter, Edda, and subsequently began an affair with her. While this relationship didn't last, the others he had with ex-Nazis Walter Rauff and Klaus Barbie continued for many years, regardless of the war crimes the pair had committed.

Heidemann's initial association with Stern was through Stern's parent company, Gruner + Jahr, who agreed to produce a book based on conversations between him and his Nazi friends. The book never materialised, leaving Heidemann no option but to borrow more money from his employers.

His attempts at selling the yacht were thwarted but resulted in him meeting Jakob Tiefenthaeler, a collector of Nazi memorabilia, who put Heidemann in touch with Stiefel, a man known for his keen interest in Göring's personal effects. It was only a matter of time before the two started sharing with one another the highlights of their collections. In early 1980, Stiefel revealed to Heidemann that he possessed the Hitler diaries. He went on to try and arrange a meeting between Heidemann and Kujau, but the latter refused to take part. Meanwhile, Heidemann approached his editor at Stern about a potential story but was rebuffed.

In the end, it was Tiefenthaeler who put Heidemann in contact with Kujau, telling him to ask for the forger under his old alias, Mr Fischer. During the resultant telephone conversation, Kujau expanded his collection to include 27 volumes of the diaries, as well as an unpublished third volume of Mein Kampf, an opera called Wieland der Schmied (Wieland the Blacksmith) and numerous letters, papers and paintings. Although Kujau refused Heinemann's initial offer of two million DMs, both parties agreed to continue to deal with each other and to do so in complete secrecy.

While neither Heidemann nor his fellow reporter Thomas Walde approached anyone at Stern, they did present an initial prospectus to the deputy managing director of parent company Gruner + Jahr, and in doing so, secured 200,000 DM as a deposit for Kujau. No historian was approached at this stage, so no validation was requested or provided.

Heinemann was a man on a mission, living up to his journalistic pseudonym the Bloodhound, earned through his tendency to investigate far beyond the needs of an article, leaving other writers to complete the story from his copious piles of notes. As Heidemann and Kujau entered into a series of negotiations, Heidemann offered Kujau a uniform which he claimed had belonged to Goring, while Kujau handed over a painting ostensibly by Hitler himself. Both items proved to be faked.

At around the same time, some of the poems Kujau had sold as authored by Hitler were beginning to have a shadow of doubt cast over them by their publishers. One historian pointed out that a poem included in the publication had actually been written by Herybert Menzel. Doubts over the authenticity of other items in Stiefel's collection also came to light, but Kujau extricated himself from the situation, saying that they had come from a source with whom he no longer had any dealings. The doubts seemingly pushed Kujau to greater heights, and within 10 days of the meeting with his publishers, he had completed three further diaries and scheduled himself to write three more each month, with some being finished in a matter of days.

The prolific amount of work on offer helped convince the parties involved of its authenticity. After all, who would or could create so many handwritten volumes in such a short space of time?

The first three diaries secured an initial deal between Heidemann and Kujau, although Heidemann handed over considerably less than the 40,000 DMs he had promised for each diary. Heidemann took a commission of 10% and held back further funds because an expert was needed to validate the diaries, after which he would pay the balance due.

Secrecy often has a role to play in cons and scams and never more so than in this instance. This was a journalistic scoop of note, but should it become common knowledge, it would no longer pack such a punch. Therefore not only were the editors left out of the loop, but it was also agreed that verification of the documents should only be sought once the entire collection had been secured.

While the handing over of the diaries continued, Heidemann acquired his own contract with Gruner + Jahr which gave him both access to the diaries after their publication and a bonus of 300,000 DMs, most of which was spent on the refurbishment of his Goring yacht.

In this particular scenario, forger and fraudster were not the same people. While Kujau scribbled away creating Hitler's work, Heidemann used his "domineering personality" to dupe his investors into paying more than he passed on to his source, securing for himself around 300,000 DMs in the process.

Breaking his own vow of secrecy, Heidemann showed one of the diaries to a friend of his, former SS general Wilhelm Mohnke, who had been in the regiment mentioned in one or two of the entries. According to the diary, Hitler had visited the barracks of Lichterfelde and Friesenstraße on specific dates, but Mohnke recalled that Hitler had never been to Friesenstraße and the regiment was only given the name SS Leibstandarte Adolf Hitler later in the Nazi campaign.

Heidemann was indifferent to his friend's testimony and in the opinion of journalist Robert Harris, "had long ceased operating on a rational wavelength about the diaries".

As the diary purchases continued, so the number of people knowing of their existence expanded and Heidemann's frivolous attitude to personal prosperity gained momentum. He informed Gruner + Jahr that the price per diary had increased from 85,000 DMs to 100,000 DMs due to the problems of smuggling them into West Germany. Kujau never saw this money, but Heidemann clearly did as his collection of Nazi memorabilia started to grow exponentially while his new BMW and Porsche cars announced to the world that he was a man of considerable means.

Heidemann's part in the fraud may not have been entirely motivated by money, and the same could perhaps be said of others who were knowingly involved. Charles Hamilton, an expert on handwriting and forgery, suggests that some were motivated by the desire to create a new Hitler – Adolf the Amiable.

The diaries revealed a Hitler who was not only uncompromising and tyrannical but also a gentleman with a loving heart, capable of blunders and moments of uncertainty. The diaries make no reference to death camps or the murder of millions of Jews, an omission which sat well with those like Heidemann who were desperate to believe in this sanitised version of the Nazi leader.

By the end of 1981, Gruner + Jahr had spent a total of 1.81 million DMs on the diaries and had 18 in their possession but still not the complete set. Inevitably, the price went up again, this time to 200,000 DMs per diary. Hitler was, it seemed, becoming increasingly prolific!

The following year, Heidemann and his sidekick Walde contacted officials at the German Federal Archives and asked them to authenticate some documents, including a page taken from one of the diaries. They provided the experts with additional samples so they could compare the handwriting in the diary to other notes ostensibly written by Hitler. Unfortunately, the samples were Kujau forgeries, which fooled the specialists into concluding that the diaries were genuine.

Confident they were headed for a journalistic tour-de-force, Stern continued to splash out on the diaries, which had now grown in number from the twenty-seven they'd originally bid for to a total of thirty-five.

Keen to maximise their readership, they invited several newspapers and magazines to meet at a vault in a Swiss bank, where they could discuss the sale of rights to other publications. Historian Hugh Trevor-Roper was asked to examine the diaries, along with a number of false positives, which led him to believe in their authenticity. He was informed that the paper on which the diaries were written had been tested and proven to be pre-war. He was also told that Stern knew the identity of the East German officer who had safeguarded the diaries following the plane crash.

All this disinformation led him to make a declaration he would undoubtedly regret for the rest of his life: "I am now satisfied that the documents are authentic... and that the standard accounts of Hitler's writing habits, of his personality, and even, perhaps, of some public events may, in consequence, have to be revised." Rupert Murdoch of News

Corporation responded immediately, arriving in Zurich the next day with his negotiating team at his side. While Murdoch made a provisional deal with Stern which would give him US serialisation rights, deals and historians continued to fly backwards and forwards.

Newsweek magazine sent historian Gerhard Weinberg to Zurich to endorse the authenticity of the diaries. He concluded that "the notion of anyone forging hundreds, even thousands of pages of handwriting was hard to credit". Although both Murdoch and the Newsweek team subsequently pulled out of negotiations, others proceeded, and news of the diaries finally broke with a press conference on 25th April 1983.

Almost immediately, historians around the world began airing their reservations about the authenticity of the documents. English historian David Irving found himself fielding calls from news companies around the world, including the BBC, The Observer and Newsweek, and was vociferous in condemning the diaries as forgeries. Hugh Trevor-Roper's own misgivings led him to make a dramatic U-turn on his previous assurances as to their authenticity. Far from the journalistic triumph, Stern had hoped their press conference would be, it turned into a farce as fingers were pointed and questions went unanswered. David Irving, who had been smuggled in by rival publication Bild to sabotage the press conference, took the microphone and asked 4 damning questions:

- Why did the forensic affidavits shown to journalists not mention the ink being laboratory tested?

- How could Hitler have continued writing his diaries after the July 20 Bomb Plot had rendered his right hand all but useless?

- Why were there clear discrepancies in the documents accompanying the diaries?

- And why had the editors of Stern refused to sign a written guarantee that the diaries were genuine?

Rather than answer these questions, the Stern representatives ordered the microphone switched off. This led to some pushing and shoving between journalists, which in turn led to punches being thrown. In the midst of it all, Irving was ejected from the conference, but not before his mischief had been done.

The stakes had now changed for the editors at Stern. They had gone from being on the brink of an epic scoop to facing charges relating to the dissemination of Nazi propaganda. The legal department at Stern leapt into action and sent three of the diaries to Dr Henke at Bundesarchiv for a complete examination.

While the controversy raged on, Heidemann secured the last four diaries from Kujau, apparently indifferent to the scandal that was about to bust wide open. At the other end of the scale, Irving continued to flip-flop on his theories, telling The Daily Express that he believed the diaries to be real – just six days after having publicly refuted that exact point. Whatever the outcome, his reputation would never be the same again.

Irving based his new position on the fact that Hitler had been diagnosed with Parkinson's disease and the handwriting in the diary from April 1945 sloped downwards and decreased in size towards the end of each line, which is consistent with the handwriting of someone with this condition. A serial holocaust denier, Irving found the lack of any reference to the Final Solution consistent with his belief that Hitler knew nothing of these atrocious events.

Irving's theories were all well, and good but forensic evidence told a different story. Ultraviolet light had revealed fluorescence in the paper which would not have been present in a pre-war diary. Not only that but the polyester in the bindings indicated they must have been manufactured after 1953.

Despite this onslaught of bad news, Stern remained resolute and defiant. Rather than accept the findings and admit their mistake, they searched for alternative explanations as to how post-war chemicals could have ended up on wartime paper. Unfortunately for them, further examination drove nail after nail into the coffin they'd built themselves, and they were eventually faced with no option but to admit the diaries were not only forgeries but poor ones at that. All along, handwriting expert Kenneth W. Rendell had been convinced the diaries were fake, and he was now able to crow that these "terrible renditions" of Hitler's handwriting and signature indicated that "the forger failed to observe or to imitate the most fundamental characteristics of his handwriting."

To limit the damage, Stern attempted to release the first statement to the press stating unequivocally that the diaries were fake but were pipped at the post by the West German government. The aftermath of the statement led to the resignation of editors Koch and Schmidt and left the magazine struggling to regain its reputation for over a decade. While Kujau had initially fled to Austria, news reports stating that Stern had paid nine million DM for the diaries (a far greater amount than he had actually received) angered him so much that he promptly phoned a lawyer and agreed to hand himself in. Bitterness and resentment towards Heidemann inspired Kujau to confess all and to declare – almost certainly dishonestly – that Heidemann had always known the diaries were fake.

A lengthy police investigation and a court case ensued in which Heidemann and Kujau were both charged with defrauding Stern of 9.3 million DM. Despite the seriousness of the charges, the court case often descended into a slanging match between the two accused.

After a year-long trial, Heidemann was found guilty of stealing 1.7 million DMs from Stern and sentenced to four years and eight months in prison while Kujau was found guilty of receiving 1.5 million DMs and was imprisoned for four years and six months. In effect, this meant over five million DMs were left unaccounted for.

The sentences passed by Judge Hans-Ulrich Schroeder were not as severe as might have been expected, and he explained that he had softened the sentences in recognition of Stern's negligence. Kujau was released from prison in 1987 when it was discovered he was suffering from throat cancer. He continued working as a forger - this time signing all his paintings with his own name - and even made forgeries of his own forgeries, reproducing some of the paintings he had previously attributed to Hitler's brushwork. Despite his new career being lucrative, he was soon back to his old ways and was arrested for falsifying driving licenses. Kujau passed away in 2000.

As for Heidemann, according to the little information available, he continues to live on in near-poverty and with accusations hanging over him that he was a spy for the Germans during the 1950s, despite his vehement denials.

Leaving the money factor to one side, the journalistic, political and historical significance of the diaries seems to have blurred the vision of almost all involved. Brian McArthur, who was working for the *Sunday Times* while the fiasco was underway, says "the discovery of the Hitler diaries offered so tempting a scoop that we all wanted to believe they were genuine."

Stern editor Schmidt wrote that everyone wanted to believe someone else was taking ultimate responsibility both for the authenticity of the diaries and for the story itself. In retrospect, it is easy to be shocked by the ridiculous level of secrecy that those involved found themselves embroiled in and the "illegitimate mystification" surrounding the affair. Many feel such an event could never be repeated, not least because the fascination with Hitler hasn't passed down to later generations for whom he has not played a major role in shaping their lives.

Dr Harald Welzer, a social psychologist, claims that the Germans have since acknowledged national guilt surrounding the events of the Holocaust and that this has helped to release them from their fixation with the man who instigated it all. The diaries have survived the ordeal and are now, ironically, secured in a history museum located in Bonn, from where Heidemann has tried to get them back, so far without success.

# BRE X MINERALS

There's an old adage that says, "All that glitters is not gold" and
there is no situation where this carries more weight than in the gold scandal
of Bre-X in the mid-1990s. Not only did the Indonesian location promise
great returns of the much-coveted yellow metal, it was in a remote jungle
setting that added mystery and romance to the discovery. Who could resist?
Well, certainly not the stockbrokers who had a field day watching Bre-X
shares soar up the stock market as though rocket-powered. Sadly, Bre-X
shares obeyed Newton's Universal Law of Gravity and plummeted as
quickly as they skyrocketed, leaving many with empty pockets and broken
dreams.

Beginning at the beginning, however, we find a desperate prospector
running a penny-stock mining company out of his Canadian basement.
Having followed in his father's and grandfather's stockbroking footsteps,
David Walsh had had little success in either oil or gas and, in 1989,
established the Bre-X mining company in a death-throe attempt at
establishing his fortune. Within three years, however, his exploration

attempts had yielded nothing, and he declared personal bankruptcy. Without even a couple of cents to rub together, Walsh's company was barely in existence being, as he described it as "a shell of a company with an almost non-existent working capital". Quite what inspired him to head to Indonesia is hard to say – a dream, an idea – but off he went with the sum total of $6,900 and a firm belief that the jungle contained his future fortune.

Busang is situated in the East Kalimantan region in Indonesia and is known as the "national coffer" due to the mineral riches hidden deep in its forests. From oil and gas to coal and gold, it's no wonder Kalimantan is described as "the land of hope". While the Busang mine is clouded in controversy, other mines in the area proved impressively productive. The Kelinan mine was discovered in 1976 and, following twelve years of exploration, produced almost twice the amount of gold indicated by the original feasibility study before it closed in 2004. In addition to productive mines, there is evidence that suggests the local Dayak tribe had been successfully panning the rivers for gold for centuries. According to researcher and academic Professor Stanley J. O'Connor, the country seemingly abounded in gold in the early 19th century, but the precious metal was considered less valuable than edible birds' nests! He notes that an explorer by the name of Dalton observed that gold dust was available only in small quantities, despite the proliferation of the substance in the local area. Dalton suggested that "it may be got in larger parcels, but the gathering of the nests has in great measure impeded the transportation of normal supplies." In retrospect, maybe the ambitious prospectors would have had more success in farming bird nests than mining gold!

So, while it would appear Walsh was on something of a wild goose chase, there was concrete evidence of gold deposits in the area – he just needed an experienced geologist to find them. Enter the mysterious and charismatic Filipino Michael de Guzman. An intelligent man with 10 years' mining experience, de Guzman had joined the many other Filipino miners who flocked to Indonesia in search of higher wages. A well-respected geologist with a passion for his work, de Guzman was seeking recognition as well as a higher-paying job. Certain that he and fellow geologist, John Felderhof, had located a huge gold deposit in the wilds of Borneo, the two men invited Walsh to a meeting in Indonesia, convincing him that Busang was the answer to his prayers. Felderhof had considerable credentials, having uncovered a large deposit of gold in Papua New Guinea some 25 years previously, and gave substance to de Guzman's rather wild claims.

With Walsh's first minimal investment, Felderhof and de Guzman set to work, established a rough-hewn settlement deep in the forest and started drilling. With shacks cobbled together from wooden planks and local villagers sweating over the drills in excruciating heat and humidity, the three men pursued their dream. While the initial results were far from encouraging, de Guzman begged Felderhof to keep trying. According to de Guzman, "In December 1993, John said, 'Close the property,' and then we made the hit." Even though the initial exploratory holes had produced nothing and other prospectors in the area were also coming up empty-handed, de Guzman and Felderhof stuck to their guns, eventually "proving" the existence of what mining analysts called, "the gold find of the century".

Bre-X Minerals was literally sitting on a gold mine – or so everyone believed. The Canadian company enjoyed an unprecedented ascent up the stock markets, leaping from 30 cents to $170 per share in just two years. While some investors were reticent about plunging their money into a far distant hole in the ground, others were more than happy to part with their hard-earned cash in the hopes of hitting the jackpot. One particular investor, Arlen Thompson, bought into both Bre-X and Bresea, Walsh's Montreal Stock Exchange Company that owned around a quarter of Bre-X. According to Thompson, Bre-X was "the Cinderella stock of the century". A highly successful stockbroker, Thompson was convinced of Bre-X's strength, despite the doubts voiced by his rivals. Leading broker for Levesque Securities, Angus Watt, had bought Bre-X shares in the early days but quickly sold them on for a small profit, saying he was uncomfortable with the company's meteoric rise. "Bull's profit," he recited, "bears profit, and little piggies get slaughtered." In retrospect, Watt was something of a fortune teller.

Nevertheless, looking at Bre-X's situation at the time, Thompson was right in his observation that "...American Barrick, the world's third-largest gold producer, has more than 350 million shares outstanding and trades at $42. It's gold reserves are 38 million ounces. Bre-X, on the other hand, has been quoted to have more than 40 million ounces of gold and has only 24 million shares outstanding. And it still has lots of exploring to do . . ." It looked and sounded like a safe bet, but looks can be deceiving!

For some of those on the ground in Busang, their suspicions that all was not quite as it seemed were aroused fairly early in the exploratory process. One of the local drilling operators, Ian, recalls having seen yellow rock pulled out of the ground during the initial investigations in 1995. Despite this promising indication, the sample was hidden away, and the hole subsequently filled in. Soon after, the area yielding the yellow stone was closed altogether and Ian, along with other workers, was sent to explore a new location. Perplexed, Ian discovered that the new site, Busang II, bore only green stone, "Such rock has no gold" he says. Ian felt that Bre-X was failing in its duties to produce a valid feasibility study, "I hoped Busang or Bre-X would still do exploration, but the fact was they manipulated the data".

Other geologists working at Busang were also sceptical about some of the practices being implemented by Bre-X. In the movie based on the Bre-X saga, Gold, all the core samples are packed into bags and sealed with wax before they leave the site. However, in reality, many sample packages were left open even while being stored in an office in the nearby city of Samarinda. Open samples are vulnerable to contamination, but the practice was defended by some of the more senior geologists on the site, who claimed the bags needed to remain open into order to preserve the quality of the rock inside and to prevent the bags from splitting open.

Despite these unconventional practices, news of the speculation that the Busang site contained as much as 200 million ounces of gold created a gold rush all of its own, with every conceivable player wanting a piece of the pie. From major gold companies to dodgy politicians, Bre-X seeming had free rein when it came to choosing their partners. However, the influence of the corrupt Indonesian government soon saw an end to that and their threats to seize the enter mine and its secret treasures resulted in Bre-X agreeing to go into production with a New Orleans-based company, Freeport McMoRan Copper and Gold Inc.

This wasn't the best move for Bre-X, and the company soon saw its shares take a considerable hit as their share in Busang was cut from 90% to 45%, with Freeport taking a 15% share and some Indonesian entities the rest. In effect, this was the beginning of the end. As part of the agreement, Freeport was keen to carry out its own exploratory digs on the Busang site and flew out in early 1997, just as de Guzman joined other Bre-X executives to attend a mining conference in Toronto.

De Guzman was reportedly in high spirits, despite having written to his mother to say he was frightened for his life. In his letter, de Guzman wrote, "Pray for me mom, they want to kill me." Suffering from both hepatitis B and malaria, de Guzman's state of mind seemed to be deteriorating, and colleagues said he exhibited increasingly unpredictable behaviour. Despite these reports, de Guzman wined and dined with the best of them during his time in Toronto, frequenting a strip club called For Your Eyes Only and embarking on the seduction of one of the club's exotic dancers.

Delving further into de Guzman's background, one wonders just how stable he had been in the years before the windfall of Busang. With four wives dotted around the globe, de Guzman was somehow juggling four families, none of whom had any knowledge of the others. Also, he was spending vast swathes of time in the jungle hunting for minerals. Nevertheless, while in Canada, de Guzman seemed keen to add another to his harem, and unsuccessfully proposed to the Toronto-based exotic dancer shortly before heading back to Indonesia to meet with Freeport-McMoRan representatives to discuss their findings.

The night before he was due to leave Canada, de Guzman had been enjoying the city nightlife, belting out tunes at a local karaoke restaurant. However, the following morning de Guzman asked his co-workers to find him some new clothes as his were quite wet. He claimed he had fallen asleep in the bath after having consumed a bottle of cough medicine. He told Bre-X colleague, Rudy Vega that this wasn't the first time and admitted, "I should not have done this". Vega later contested that "It was my impression Michael had tried to commit suicide that night." Certainly, the ongoing symptoms of hepatitis, including stomach aches, painful joints, nausea and fatigue may have pushed de Guzman to the limit but, surely, with several million to his name, he had everything to live for.

What follows deepens the mystery. Suicide, murder, accidental death – will we ever really know the answer? Some four hours after his conversation with Vega, de Guzman was on board a helicopter destined for Busang and what could prove a rather volatile meeting with the disgruntled officials from Freeport. According to pilot Edy Torsono, after approximately twenty minutes in the air he heard a loud bang and, on looking over his shoulder, saw the door was open, and de Guzman was gone.

It took several days to find the body in the thick Indonesian jungle and, once recovered, there was little to positively identify it as anything more than human. Decomposition was accelerated by the hot and humid conditions, while leeches, maggots and wild boar alike had made the most of this unexpected airdrop. Nevertheless, Vega was convinced the body belonged to de Guzman as it was clothed in the same items he had secured for his colleague that morning, following the bath incident. Similarly, one of his more recent wives, Lilis de Guzman, positively identified the body by photographs of the corpse. "There is no uncertainty," she said, "I believe he is dead."

Shortly after de Guzman's body plummeted some 800 feet into the Indonesian jungle, so Bre-X's shares went into freefall. On March 20, 1997, a few days after de Guzman's death, Walsh answered reporters' questions, saying, "There are all sorts of rumours going around, but we're waiting for the investigation to take its course,". In a Calgary Herald article, Stephen Ewart observed that de Guzman's death had an instant effect on share prices, knocking them down by 40 cents within days. Nevertheless, mining analysts believed Bre-X would soon bounce back and "de Guzman's death shouldn't have a long-term impact." How wrong they proved to be!

In the surreal few days that followed, rumours abounded and a report from an Indonesian newspaper suggesting the deposits at the Busang mine may be considerably smaller than initially thought and "may not be worth mining at all" hit Bre-X's shares like a wrecking ball. In one day, more than nine million shares were bought and sold, and de Guzman's suicide seemed increasingly more likely to be related to the unproductivity of the mine rather than his ill health.

According to mining analyst at a reputable Vancouver-based company, Richard Cohen, "So far these are just unsubstantiated rumours, but it's easy to understand why investors are nervous... There are billions of dollars at stake here, and we're being hit with one thing after another." On the morning of Friday 21st March, trading in Bre-X shares was frozen after they had slumped to rock-bottom as a result of de Guzman's death and reports that Freeport studies showed Busang was unlikely to produce an economic gold mine.

At the time, mining analysts said the connection between the suggested anomalies in the Busang sampling project and de Guzman's death was "inconceivable", with one senior mining analyst, Dorothy Atkinson, stating, "there are these false pictures being painted behind the tragedy... I think it's just a totally false article based on the personal tragedy of de Guzman." While speculation about de Guzman's death continued, so did concerns about the potential productivity of the Busang site and, to put the rumours to bed, Bre-X hired an independent consultant, Strathcona Mineral Services of Toronto, to explore the area and confirm its potential. Sadly, Strathcona failed to consolidate Bre-X's hopes and dreams, concluding that "there is virtually no possibility of an economic gold deposit".

Strathcona's findings were damning for Bre-X, revealing that the drilling samples had been interfered with and, in effect, 'salted'. In other words, gold from other sources had been added into the core samples to create the impression of a productive supply of the precious metal when, in fact, there was little more than fool's gold and worthless dust. It was later revealed that core samples were contaminated with shavings from jewellery and gold panned from the nearby rivers.

While salting is hardly a new concept, dating back to colonial America when salt was a highly sought-after commodity, salting on this scale was almost unthinkable. The simplicity of it was exceptional, especially on an international scale, and the difference between panned gold and mined gold should have been obvious to those examining the core samples. In the movie, Gold, the character based on David Walsh says that no one noticed because no one was looking. Everyone wanted to believe in the dream, so no one looked too hard at the evidence. Very like the Hitler Diaries, in fact – Stern *wanted* them to be real and so didn't look hard enough for evidence that they might not be.

A fabulous confidence trick that turned some into millionaires and other into paupers, the court case involving Bre-X continued for seventeen years before being dismissed by an Ontario judge on the basis that any remaining profits for the scam had been squandered on the enormous legal fees involved in the case. Felderhof was the only person to face charges and was believed to have benefited to the sum of $84 million from his part in the Bre-X scandal. He has consistently denied any knowledge of or involvement in the fraud.

It is not only the scandal and court case that remained in the headlines for over a decade after the event, with speculation around de Guzman's death continuing for some 10 years after his demise. Inconclusive evidence has led some to believe that de Guzman is still alive and well, living in some far-flung location, enjoying the fruits of his dubious labours. According to one of his four wives, de Guzman made a deposit of $100,000 into her account five years after his so-called suicide, adding fuel to the rumours that he may still be alive.

The speculation around de Guzman's death was sparked by the authorities who struggled to correctly establish the identity of the badly decomposed body retrieved from the jungle. The Philippines' National Bureau of Investigation battled to match the corpse's fingerprints with those on record as Michael de Guzman, and some of those involved in the initial autopsy are still sceptical and uncertain or the corpse's true identity. While de Guzman's close family remain convinced that de Guzman committed suicide on that fateful day in Indonesian, a further report issued by investigators into his death indicates that de Guzman was murdered.

Anthropologist Jerome Bailen enjoys a heady amount of respect and has been dubbed the Philippines' answer to Sherlock Holmes. According to Bailen and his team, marks found on the neck and back of the body retrieved from the jungle indicate that de Guzman had been tortured before his death. They say the marks show evidence of de Guzman being strangled and claim that the Indonesian military abducted him, hoping to find out the truth behind the Busang mine. The body they examined, believed to have been de Guzman's, was missing internal organs and genitalia which the original autopsy attributed to animals feeding on the body before it was found. Bailen claims the body was desecrated prior to being thrown from the helicopter.

Further evidence that de Guzman was murdered, Bailen says, is obvious from the documents found in the helicopter and his hotel room after his death. These supposed suicide notes contain some misspellings and grammatical errors that are incongruous given de Guzman's command of the English language. The report suggests that these errors may have been "...de Guzman's way of signalling that the large scrawling he wrote – or was 'made to write' – on the yellow pad paper were not earnestly his..." In summation, the report concludes that "The real cause and manner of the death of Mr Michael de Guzman could never be ruled as suicide."

In contrast to these findings, the Indonesian police concluded de Guzman's death was suicide – a hypothesis that was backed up by the Royal Canadian Mounted Police who travelled to Indonesia to review the incident. Mountie Perry Kuzman is on record as saying, "There wasn't anything in my mind that indicated anything other than suicide."

Sadly, there is little chance the truth will out, and family members of the deceased de Guzman are becoming tired of the constant rumour-mongering with his brother Jojo saying, "I really wish I could speak with him and ask him what really happened... I don't think we've ever known the truth".

Despite his family's fatalistic outlook, there are others that remain convinced that de Guzman is alive and well with reported sightings still trickling in from time to time. Perhaps part of the determination to believe that de Guzman stills lives and breathes is the hope that he will one day be brought to justice and those who lost their fortunes on Bre-X will be reimbursed and compensated for their loss.

Unfortunately for Canada, the scandal did little to improve the rather sketchy reputation carried by the Vancouver Stock Exchange which, in 1989, was described by Forbes magazine as the "scam capital of the world." Regrettably, many of the loopholes and flaws in the Canadian stock exchange have still not been addressed, and the police still struggle to scrape together the necessary resources to track large funds and financial scams. According to a 2005 article published on the Canadian Encyclopaedia website, Michael de Guzman will continue to live on in the collective memory of the Canadians exploited by the scam, "Is Michael de Guzman dead or alive? Our abiding interest gives the answer. He is alive and well, living the high life somewhere... in our minds at least, if not in reality."

Meanwhile, David Walsh is safely under the ground with very few suppositions or theories surrounding his demise. As depicted by Matthew McConaughey in the movie, Gold, Walsh was an overweight, chain-smoking drinker who died in 1998 at the age of 52, following a massive stroke. Despite having fled to the Bahamas to escape the scandal, the pressure of the impending lawsuits did nothing for Walsh's health or state of mind. Walsh maintained his innocence until the day he died, despite a series of lawsuits and furious accusations from investors. According to Clint Docken, a lawyer who represented two hundred of the speculators who lost money in the Bre-X scandal, Walsh knew more than he would reveal. "David had a story to tell, and we may not fully hear that story, and that's unfortunate," Docken said the day before Walsh passed away. The remaining survivor of the Bre-X scandal, John Felderhof, was last seen living out his days in the Cayman Islands with his wife.

For the Dayak tribe of Indonesia, the story is far from dead and buried, however, and the search for gold continues. Ten years after the Bre-X scandal erupted, local speculators continue to pursue the dream with rudimentary equipment and a large serving of optimism and hope. Reporter Suzanne Wilton says the process of extracting the gold is even more tortuous than the journey to Busang, which takes between a day and a week and involves a complication of road, river and hiking through dangerous jungle terrain.

The gentleman now heading up one of the local mining projects, Hasyim Asyari, earns around $250 a month for his efforts which include the arduous process of crushing the rock using a combination of "six drums connected by large rubber belts to a wobbly wheel [and a] gas-powered generator." After this, the mixture is combined with liquid mercury to bind the gold, washed with water and strained through a handkerchief. The resulting nugget is then cleansed with a blowtorch to remove impurities, leaving enough of the precious metal to earn the workers around $50. Not much for a day of slaving in scorching temperatures and 100% humidity.

According to some of the locals who worked with de Guzman and his team at the Busang site, this was the perfect location for both the romantic notion of an undiscovered field of gold and to start what Wilton describes as "a tampering scheme of unprecedented proportions." During an interview with Wilton, Benny Wahju, the former executive of the Indonesian Mining Association, acknowledges, "Limited access adds more to the mystery. It gives you a romantic touch.". Wahju goes on to say the location was perfect for the unscrupulous, "It's remote. It's unknown. The government is corrupt. You can bribe everybody to justify your story,".

Nevertheless, over the past 10 years, the rudimentary mining efforts of the locals have reportedly produced approximately 10 kilograms of gold, and even some Bre-X collaborators still believe in the area's potential. Felderhof has been reported as saying the evidence produced to prove Busang lacking in gold was insubstantial and those who investigated the area "inept". One of the Indonesian businessmen involved in the original Busang scandal still maintains there is gold there – the only real question is, how much? According to Ahmad Syakerani, there is still enough potential to warrant international investment, "If there is someone interested in continuing the Busang project," he says, "please come to Indonesia. Do not hesitate, because there is gold in that area."

While Syakerani still hopes for another Canadian investor, it's unlikely any Canadian would be willing to step forward and prospect the area again. There are ghosts aplenty surrounding Busang – both real and imagined – and the likelihood of being laughed out of the boardroom and persecuted on the streets is pretty high. While Kalimantan may remain the "land of hope" for some, it's unlikely any Canadian prospectors will be heading that way with the collective Canadian memory unwilling to forget the humiliation and financial devastation that ensued from the last forays into the Indonesian jungle.

Regardless of whether de Guzman is alive or dead, his legacy will live on for some time to come. And his motive? According to Strathcona president, Graham Farquharson, the desire to preserve his high-ranking job motivated de Guzman who had failed to gain the recognition he felt he deserved as a geologist, despite his intelligence and diligence. Other theories posit that the Filipino mafia was at the core of the hoax and subsequently murdered de Guzman to safeguard their secrets. Still, others suggest the corrupt President of Indonesia, Suharto, was instrumental in seeing Bre-X collapse to take control over the gold deposit for his own profits. This seems unlikely as further activity in the Busang area has been limited to the embryonic efforts of local villagers. A further theory, which is even more outrageous, suggests that Walsh is also still alive, having faked his death and that he and de Guzman are living like kings, enjoying their ill-gotten gains in some obscure corner of the world.

Whatever the truth, it seems some are unwilling to let the story die even as the passing years make the protagonists' survival increasingly unlikely. Maybe they are fuelled by the possibility of one day regaining those lost investments, or maybe the pure romance and adventure of the whole affair make it hard to let go.

# BERNIE MADOFF

Charles Dickens was ahead of his time when he first outlined the idea for a pyramid-style financial scam in 1844 in his novel, Martin Chuzzlewit, although a Brooklyn bookkeeper by the name of William F. Miller used a similar scheme just over 50 years later to swindle investors out of $1m. Maybe it was one of these early ideas that inspired Bernie Madoff to create one of the largest Ponzi schemes the world has ever known. Running for several decades, with hundreds if not thousands of victims, and a grand total of $64-million, Madoff certainly pulled off one of the biggest scams in history.

How you judge the success of a pyramid scheme is hard to gauge but if it is reflected in the quantity of money diverted then there has been nothing to even contest Madoff who succeeded in taking over 50 times more from his victims than the famous Ponzi himself. Madoff's story begins like many others, and his high standing and reputation within the financial industry gave him the capacity to convince big names to give him even larger amounts of money. From Steven Spielberg to John Malkovich and Zsa Zsa Gabor, Madoff's list of victims is star-studded and as exclusive as they come but, then, who wouldn't trust a man who was advising the Securities and Exchange Commission on trading precautions?

In keeping with the so-called rules of a Ponzi scheme, Madoff promised clients impressive returns on their investments and then encouraged them to leave their money where it was to accumulate even higher yields. While his strategies were typically vague, his assurance was enough for many, and the high level of exclusivity surrounding the speculation helped Madoff tempt a long list of new investors, keeping his scheme alive longer than most could have anticipated. Like many Ponzi schemes, however, when Madoff's investment scam crashed, it took more than just his fortune and freedom with it; it estranged him from his sons, exiled his wife from the friends he had betrayed and left his family reeling in tragedy and financial disaster. Madoff paid for his greed and betrayal with more than just his 150-year prison sentence.

Bernie Madoff was exposed in late 2008 when he admitted that the wealth management arm of his Wall Street firm, Bernard L. Madoff Investment Securities LLC, was, in fact, a complicated Ponzi scheme. How long it had been running is hard to say, although Madoff subsequently admitted that he hadn't really traded since the early 1990s. Other sources believe this particular division of his firm had been fraudulent from the start, indicating that Madoff managed to keep his scheme afloat for over 30 years! This longevity is unusual in a typical Ponzi scheme as the inability to draw new investors soon sees the whole thing collapse, but Madoff was also managing money for charities which enabled him to dodge the threats of sudden or unpredictable withdrawals. Furthermore, with his brokerage operation a real entity in the world of investments, Madoff was in a very different position from other Ponzi schemes that base their strategies on non-existent businesses.

Whatever else Madoff may have been, he was definitely not stupid, and the strategy he sold to his clients (or victims) consisted of the buying of blue-chip stocks coupled with taking options contracts on them. It was partly the scheme's surprising success that first lead to suspicions that all wasn't as it seemed. Harry Markopolos was one of the first to smell a rat. As a portfolio manager at Rampart Investment Management, Markopolos was instructed to design a product that would replicate Madoff's returns. Markopolos put in his best effort but, after four hours, concluded that Madoff's sums just didn't add up. The mathematics at the crux of Madoff's strategies simply didn't work, making Markopolos believe that either Madoff was using information from his clients to buy stock for his own account or he was running the biggest Ponzi scheme in the world.

Not only would Madoff's exposure damage his family name but, with so many relations working alongside him, it opened up a can of worms that all his family had to wrestle with. Inevitably, having his brother, sons and niece all working within his firm meant that, after his own arrest, suspicion moved swiftly to his family members, even though his sons had been integral in exposing the scam in the first place. One of the newer members of the family, Eric Swanson who had recently married Bernie's niece, Shana, came under particularly exacting scrutiny. Eric and Shana met in 2003 when Shana was working for Bernard L. Madoff Investment Securities LLC as the compliance lawyer and Swanson was an official for the Securities and Exchange Commission. Eric was examining the firm to ascertain whether Bernie was front running customer orders and, in the process, managed to completely overlook the multi-billion-dollar scheme running at the company's heart. The oversight seemed to be inexplicable although it later transpired that Swanson's involvement with the Madoff firm was rather minor and ceased altogether after his relationship with Shana began in 2006. Furthermore, before their relationship, Swanson was pursuing an enforcement action against another firm whose board members included his future father-in-law – Bernie's brother.

After his arrest, Bernie declared that he had acted on his own and any implications directed at his family were false. Bernie's sons both worked for him in the New York office's trading arm and were estranged from both him and their mother, Ruth, from the time of their father's arrest. While some believed this was simply a strategy to avoid their assets being caught up in the litigation, other evidence suggests that the two brothers were cut from a different cloth to their father. Both Andrew and Mark maintained, until their deaths, that they knew nothing of the scheme until their father confessed to them in December 2008 when he told them he was "finished" and they subsequently reported him to the authorities. In an interview with People magazine in 2013, Andrew said: "We never hesitated. The decision was at the same time the easiest decision I ever had to make and the hardest." Andrew died of cancer in September 2014 while his brother, Mark, apparently traumatised by the scandal, took his own life on the second anniversary of his father's arrest.

According to friends of the brothers, as reported by David Margolick, a Vanity Fair writer, Andrew has described his father's actions as "a father-son betrayal of biblical proportions" while others still maintain that their purported innocence is, quite simply, unbelievable. In both his article and his interviews, Margolick posits the possibility that the sons have merely been acting, to which the answer is, always: "Yes, it's possible". It takes a fair stretch of the imagination and some impressive amateur dramatics on the sons' side for it to be believable. Apparently, neither of the sons spoke to their father again, and relations with their mother weren't much better, although not because they suspected her of being involved in the scam, but because, Margolick reports, they believed her unswayable loyalty to her husband had aided and abetted him to some degree. During his interviews, Margolick spoke with Bernie's ex-private secretary, Eleanor Squillari, who observed the sons for the twenty years she spent in Bernie's employ. She noted that the relationship between father and sons was less than straightforward. While he doted on them, he also resented the fact that he had provided them with everything on a plate – a silver spoon in their mouths, so to speak. Did he throw everything away just so his sons could experience the struggle he had?

Madoff was a master marketer and reinvented himself from his Queens' upbringing to a Wall Street giant. After graduating with a Bachelor of Arts in political science from Hofstra University in 1960, Bernie promptly established his own company, Bernard L. Madoff Investment Securities LLC, with the $5000 he saved from his odd jobs as a sprinkler system installer and a lifeguard. Nevertheless, it wasn't all that tough going from then on as his generous father-in-law gave him a $50,000 loan with which to further develop his company. The notion that he was hoping to force some mettle out of his sons by way of his scandal is far-fetched, to say the least.

Bernie and Ruth were apparently inseparable during their courting days and, as the daughter of accountant Saul Alpern, Ruth also did some bookkeeping for her husband in the early years of his entrepreneurial business. To date, there has been no proof that Ruth knew anything about her husband's $65-billion scheme and she has escaped prosecution. Not to say she hasn't suffered, however, losing both her sons and having her considerable assets frozen on top of seeing her husband imprisoned for the rest of his life, would take its toll on anyone. Her loyalty to her husband goes unquestioned, though, which is interesting when you consider the perspective his employees had of him.

According to Squillari, Bernie was flirtatious and had a long list of "masseuses" saved in his address book which would have raised a few eyebrows had it ever been made public. He was also given to making inappropriate remarks. Former directors of Madoff's described him in intimate detail to a captivated audience in court in June 2013. From their testimonies, it becomes clear that Madoff was obsessive-compulsive with offices decorated only in black, white and grey and employees banned from having personal effects on their desks. When stressed, Madoff became nasty and was considered pretty unapproachable. Directors of his London office said he was fanatical about micro-management and wanted 24-hour surveillance on the trading floor which they found both unsettling and demeaning. Meanwhile, if anyone phoned to ask about anything that wasn't directly related to trading, his employees were instructed to forward the calls either to himself or to one of his sons – no one else was privy to certain information. Secretive and paranoid, Bernie was also the ultimate salesman, holding a velvet rope in his hands as he waited for the next prey.

Some reports are at odds with the clear evidence that Bernie was respected and accepted by the people who invested with him. Bernie's scheme amounts to a form of affinity fraud, although others posit that he was never truly part of the Upper East Side clan in which he existed. According to some, he remained the desperate progeny of some unknown ancestry in Queens and could never really understand the unspoken rules of New York's upper-middle class. Nevertheless, Bernie succeeded in using his Jewish ancestry to convince members of the moneyed American Jewish communities. Bernie's charm extended to the opposite sex as well, and he's described as being "irresistible to women".

Not all were taken in by the man, however, and one childhood friend of Ruth's says her father warned her against investing with him 15 years before the scandal was revealed. Her husband was less fortunate, losing his accumulated wealth to the Madoff scam. Bernie was certainly a complex individual as the testimonies from various staff members indicate. Madoff's relationship with his wife is equally curious; while she would ensure she always appeared as young and beautiful as the years would allow, she also showed signs of jealousy watching her husband closely in the company of good-looking young women. Yet she would often speak to him in an angry tone, swearing and generally behaving at odds with someone of her social standing. Despite Madoff's claims, it is almost impossible to believe that

Bernie masterminded and managed one of the largest Ponzi schemes ever without any outside assistance. A securities lawyer by the name of Tom Dewey said that a fraud of this nature would require various accounting, administrative and office personnel simply to keep it afloat, while Anthony Barkow, who was once a federal prosecutor in New York stated: "Bernie Madoff claiming that he acted alone was ridiculous. His surrender was clearly a strategy to try to insulate his family and co-conspirators and made it more difficult for the government to make the case..." Bernie's unwillingness to name names made it difficult for the authorities and it took years to uncover the extent of Madoff's swindle and to reveal exactly who had known, what part they had played and how much information they were privy to.

After a six-month court case, one of the longest in history for a white-collar crime, 15 people were either convicted or pleaded guilty to their involvement with the fraud which wiped out the wealth of hundreds of people and charities. Five employees attempted to convince a jury that, while they were willing to admit they had played a part in the scam, they didn't know quite what they were involved in. Most had been in Bernie's employ for decades and claimed they had been duped, just as the investors had been. The jury was dubious, however, and disregarded their defence which hung, rather tenuously, on the assertion that "Nobody knew what he was doing,". One of the defence lawyers, Andrew Frisch, said: "These are uneducated, or thinly educated, functionaries who basically see him as a god."

The sentences were almost absurdly lenient, and it's believed this is due to this defence strategy. While Bernie received a heavy sentence of 150 years in prison, his seconds in command, brother Peter and back-office director Daniel Bonventre, received 10-year sentences, while the Chief Financial Officer, Frank DiPascali cooperated with the investigation and died before he could be sentenced. While the prosecution of the 15 other people involved in Bernie's massive deception couldn't have happened without Frank's testimony, nor could the scam itself. Frank had a lot to be grateful to Bernie for, having landed his first job there at the tender age of 19, from where he proceeded to attain the dizzy heights of Chief Financial Officer. While it's difficult to ascertain exactly when Frank went from being an office gofer to a co-conspirator, it's clear that his involvement in producing statements reflecting fake trades helped keep Bernie's scheme afloat.

Frank claimed he acted out of blind loyalty to Madoff, but he quickly shed that allegiance, agreeing to trade his testimony for the possibility of a more lenient sentence for his part in the crime. DiPascali went on to provide huge amounts of evidence that would condemn both his illustrious mentor and many of his colleagues. Annette Bongiorno, a secretary and portfolio manager at Madoff's, originally secured Frank's position for him and worked there alongside him from that day. Annette was sentenced to six years, and many felt this was insufficient punishment. However, in Annette's defence, she was hardly in a position to pull off a complex deception of the level needed to fool the Securities and Exchange Commission, top bankers, prosecutors and astute investors. In fact, how did they manage to overlook a crime of this magnitude, especially as original sceptic Harry Markopolos was repeatedly trying to open their eyes to it?

After his initial concerns about Madoff's investment strategy in 1999, Markopolos refused to be put off by the SEC's continual dismissal of his suspicions and subsequently dedicated himself to the case, tracking Madoff for over eight years and sending numerous notices to the SEC. Still, nothing happened. Similarly, while sophisticated, the premise of Madoff's swindle lacks the intricacies that would have made it truly undetectable – so how did it continue for so many years? A journalist for the Rolling Stone, Matt Taibbi, wrote: "It came out that Madoff had not merely stolen from his clients but not conducted any trades at all, simply bilking money in the most primitive conceivable Ponzi scheme. This meant that the SEC would have been able to uncover the fraud with even the most cursory examination at any time during the fund's existence." But this didn't happen – in fact, the authorities turned a blind eye to it all until Bernie confessed.

All of this seems rather incongruous, especially as banks and other businesses dealing with Madoff had raised concerns as far back as 1996, even before Markopolos started shouting from the rooftops. JP Morgan Chase, a global financial services firm and banking institution that was forced to pay out $2m for their involvement in Bernie's scam admitted that, when their own computer system raised alerts about Madoff's activities, the employees simply closed them down. It was only in October 2008 that the bank voiced concerns that his investment returns were, quite simply, too good to be true. It seems many within the financial industry chose to see what they wanted to see and, in doing so, ignored the big flashing red lights that were screaming away over Bernie's head. Journalist Erin Arvedlund was writing about Madoff as early as 2001 but, for some reason, nobody wanted to listen. In her 2001 article, Don't Ask, Don't Tell: Bernie Madoff Attracts Skeptics, Erin writes that the private accounts Bernie was managing, "…have produced compound average annual returns of 15% for more than a decade. Remarkably, some of the larger, billion-dollar Madoff-run funds have never had a down year." One would have thought this would raise some suspicions, spark an investigation or two, but nothing of the sort occurred.

The SEC comes out of the whole debacle looking less than squeaky clean and a complaint filed by Kathleen Furey, a lawyer employed in the New York Regional Office of the SEC, tarnishes their reputation even further. According to Furey, she and over 20 other colleagues were actively forbidden to bring cases against investment managers like Bernie, being told it was a "matter of policy". Furey suggested to her superiors that pursuing cases of this nature "may save the agency from future embarrassment." It seems she was right. Even the most perfunctory examination into the fund should have revealed Madoff's primitive scheme and saved investors billions of dollars.

One of the more positive outcomes resulting from Bernie Madoff's $65-billion scam has been the overhaul of the SEC to create a more effective protocol which offers staff 'precise guidelines' about how to identify red flags and potential violations. An investigation into the SEC's handling of the Madoff case indicated that staff lacked the necessary proficiencies to identify warning signs and subsequently recognise a possible fraud. Tips and reports are now entered on a computerised database whereas previously a written complaint might just be shoved into the back of a filing cabinet if it didn't carry much weight. If subsequent reports came in relating to the same business or broker, it was next to impossible to join the dots and form the bigger picture. "It was a sieve, basically," says Russ Ryan, a partner in a Washington law office who spent 10 years working at the SEC before 2004.

It seems very few people emerged from the Madoff scandal unscathed, although Bernie himself apparently enjoyed star status in Butner prison for his first few years there and his sizeable ego would appear to still be intact. One inmate claims many other prisoners approached Bernie for advice about their own projects and ambitions, massaging his ego and putting him on a pedestal within the penitentiary. The inmate said, "He wants to be remembered as a titan of Wall Street". Now 78, Madoff has called Federal Correctional Institution Butner Medium home for nearly 10 years but hasn't given up his money-making schemes because of imprisonment, at one time buying up all the hot chocolate available in the commissary and subsequently selling in the prison yard for a profit, effectively monopolising the prison's hot chocolate supplies. While prison life is, by necessity, not all plain sailing, with meals, toilet breaks and sleep all regulated, Butner is not a wholly unpleasant place to be either, with no bars, windows that open, a gym, a library, volleyball court, gardens and flowers and even an Indian sweat lodge!

While there is no way to paint Madoff as some kind of criminal genius, he certainly had what it takes in terms of charm and the capacity to make his investors believe they were privileged to be included into his elite club. As Erin Arvedlund discovered, Bernie was extremely secretive – bordering on paranoid – about how his investment strategies worked and encouraged his investors to remain tight-lipped on the subject as well, a move that made his group of venture capitalists seem even more exclusive. Another thing many of Bernie's investors had in common was that they were Jewish and Bernie most certainly targeted people who would trust him because they shared his heritage, culture and belief system. Schemes of this nature, in which the mastermind focuses on members of a particular religious or social group, are known as affinity crimes, and Bernie managed to create something of an affinity Ponzi system. Bernie encouraged a sense of intrigue as well as exclusivity and was reluctant to meet his investors face-to-face, thereby increasing the scheme's appeal. Madoff's list of victims includes Hollywood legends Steven Spielberg and John Malkovich, while J. Ezra Merkin was one of the more prominent promoters of Bernie's investment capabilities and assisted in directing $1.8 billion towards Madoff's firm. Madoff also targeted Jewish charities and used his Jewish status and reputation to entice various Jewish federations and hospitals, including the Elie Wiesel Foundation as well as numerous financial firms, such as HSBC and Fairfield Greenwich – an investment specialist that sent $7.5 billion into Madoff's pockets.

Madoff didn't restrict himself to strangers in his bid for new recruits to his scheme and, while his sons were officially employed in the trading arm of the New York office, they also helped the company by marketing Bernie's funds. The sons, themselves, along with Bernie, have consistently maintained they had no involvement in the scam but have, nevertheless, been exposed to a plethora of civil and legal suits in the aftermath of their father's exposure. At the time of Bernie's arrest, his two sons owed him over $30 million between them. Immediately following Bernie's arrest, the sons' assets were frozen, but that court order was subsequently dissolved shortly after which they, alongside their uncle Peter and cousin Shana, faced a civil lawsuit filed against them by Irving Picard which was dismissed because they were also victims of their relative's extensive crimes. The last suit against the Madoff sons was brought against all the directors of Madoff's British sector in 2013, at which point Mark had been dead some years following his suicide and his brother, Andrew, was critically ill with mantle cell leukaemia.

Ruth Madoff, Bernie's wife, has also seen her fair share of the inside of a courtroom, even though she chose not to attend his sentencing, the terms of which required she surrender all her possessions in return for being granted $2.5m for herself. With these funds not protected from civil litigation, Ruth has been named in some civil cases, the first of which was brought by Irving Picard in the July following her husband's imprisonment. According to records, she was reported to have received over $3 million in just six years, with the court report noting that, "Ruth Madoff was never an employee of BLMIS yet millions of dollars belonging to BLMIS and its customers found their way into her personal accounts and investments without any legitimate business purpose… simply because of her relationship with Bernard Madoff".

Considering that Ruth and Bernie's combined assets were valued at around $825 million, the $2.5 million she was granted must feel like meagre pocket money after her other estates and effects were frozen by the federal government, including a $7 million penthouse in the Upper East Side and an $11 million mansion in Palm Beach. While Ruth has remained fairly tight-lipped on the subject of her husband's crimes, she felt the need to speak out after being accused of simply not caring about what had happened to his victims. She said her silence was due to the sense of shame and betrayal but, nonetheless, she has also been perceived as one of the most hated women in New York, especially shortly after the whole scandal began to unfold.

Ruth is often seen around the city but is spurned by most of her old friends, many of whom were victims of her husband's scam. In some ways, Ruth can be seen to have suffered a greater penalty for her lack of involvement than her husband did for masterminding the operation. While he is safely in prison, Ruth must continue to show her face in public while being rebuffed by those who were once her closest friends and confidants. She gets little sympathy from those around her, however, who feel her suffering pales into insignificance in comparison to the anguish experienced by some of the victims who lost the life savings they were planning to retire on. Ruth continued to see her husband for some time after his imprisonment, stopping only when the remaining son, Andrew, gave her an ultimatum – if she wanted contact with him and her two granddaughters, all contact with Bernie had to stop. There are mixed reports about Ruth's current financial status, and she lives in a not too shabby gated community in Old Greenwich which is still a far cry from her apartment on Upper East Side. Some neighbours allege that she still lives a life of luxury while others claim she has a fairly frugal existence. Either way, having lost a husband and two sons, life can't be easy.

So, what on earth possessed Bernie to risk everything, his wealth, his business, his family and friends in the pursuit of wealth? Some say he simply couldn't face failure and, rather than admit defeat at a time when the whole US economy was wobbling, he opted to create an elaborate scheme that would continue to pay investors the returns they had come to expect from Madoff, the great investor. As with many con artists, it seems Madoff was truly convinced by his own importance and the extent of the power he wielded, making his confidence indestructible. Madoff also could convince others that they were special and incredibly smart for trusting him with their money. Even when the ugly truth was unveiled, it did little to penetrate Madoff's armour of self-confidence. When interviewed, Madoff maintains that he doesn't recall the exact moment that he went from being a legitimate investor to a con artist but most find this hard to believe.

In a phone interview with Harvard Business School professor Eugene Soltes, Madoff admits that he had a choice in the matter – no one was holding a gun to his head – and, by his own admission, he says: "It wasn't like I … was afraid of getting caught doing it…. I sort of rationalised that what I was doing was OK, that it wasn't going to hurt anybody." In retrospect, he couldn't have got much further from the truth. He admits it was partly ambition that drove him, alongside over-confidence which he had built up to a point where he felt he was indestructible. Eugene Soltes uses Madoff as something of a warning to his young pupils – a way of reminding them that a slight transgression that is perceived as a temporary Elastoplast over a small wound can blow out of context and can precipitate a decline into a much bigger dalliance with wrongdoing. While Soltes recognises Madoff's intellect, he also says it's pretty inconceivable that Bernie sat down and planned his multi-billion-dollar scheme from the start, adding: "He couldn't have planned such a long-running and extraordinarily devastating fraud in advance even if he tried."

Madoff himself calls the scenario "a comedy of errors", and Soltes draws his students' attention to this, reminding them that in a risk-taking business such as investment, the temptation to bend the rules is often there and may, in some cases, result in a positive outcome. With laws becoming outdated or curbing the innovation that enables businesses to flourish, the line is there to be crossed but, he warns, "the challenge for entrepreneurs is that the line between appropriate and illicit is often quite murky." Business often calls for an aggressive attitude, especially when there is as much at stake as Bernie Madoff had, but knowing when to pull back is also the sign of a successful entrepreneur.

While Madoff's innovation is as undeniable as his charm and ability to gain people's trust as easily as he gained their money, in the end, he crossed far over the line that distinguishes innovation from criminality. It is unlikely the US world of investment will forget Madoff in a hurry and, it seems, certain new laws and regulations have been implemented as a result of his extravagant fraud. Hopefully, both help protect other potential victims from such an unmitigated fleecing and also encourage other ambitious entrepreneurs to curb their aspirations and remain on the right side of the law. The fallout from Madoff's legacy continues today with many of his victims and their families still struggling in the aftermath of this tidal wave of illegality, betrayal and greed.

# FINAL THOUGHTS – STEVEN LAZAROFF

From ancient times to the modern era, humanity has displayed remarkable creativity by imagining, orchestrating and executing a well-choreographed script that, if properly planned, would reward the individuals involved with either a small gain in power, more influence, greater wealth or other advantages.

There are so many examples of schemes, frauds, swindles, shakedowns, grifts, flimflams, hussles and cons, that this book would have been much larger had we attempted to document them all.

Great military deceptions on battlefields throughout history alone could occupy an entire library.

Humans are really no different than other members of the animal kingdom when it comes to deception. On the contrary, nature is full of examples of creatures that carve out a little slice of heaven through their acts of deception and misdirection. More often than not, they have convinced their habitat that they are something they're not. Theirs is a game of survival. Their ability to fool one another can both secure a full stomach or avoid winding up in one.

Chimps have been observed to cry an alert to the troop when they know full well that there is no danger, in order to deceive or distract the others to allow them time to capture food or some other object of interest.

Female marsh harriers, a bird of prey, have been known to court their male counterpart to obtain his stored food. These beguiling females then proceed to fleece the unwitting males and feed the captured food to their chicks, fathered by another male.

These examples pale in comparison to what human beings can come up with, but the point is not lost. Animals of all stripes use varying forms of trickery to advance their individual agendas.

Confidence scams, deceptions and hoaxes have been a mainstay of human culture since we have started recording our history. Human beings want to believe, want to trust and want to think that they are smarter than other people.

Confidence scams typically exploit the victim's greed, vanity, lust, compassion, irresponsibility, desperation, or naïveté. Because of this variety of traits found in victims, there never really is a typical victim 'type' or 'profile'; Victims can be your mother, your sister, brother or close friend. Don't think you, yourself are above it all because you can also easily become a victim.

While writing this book, I was on a business trip to Paris and needed to catch an early morning train to Marseille. I made my way to Gare de Lyon, and upon arriving at the station, I proceeded to purchase a cup of coffee. I was about an hour early for my train, and it was a beautiful spring day, so I decided to stand outside the station to enjoy some fresh air and some much-needed sun.

As I was standing outside the station, leaning against a wall, browsing through the day's news on my phone, I noticed out of the corner of my eye a raggedly dressed man walking in my general direction. He wasn't walking directly at me, it was more like he was going to pass me by like countless others had before him.

My danger senses were not raised because he wasn't a threat. There were hundreds of people around me, and I felt totally safe. As he walked by, directly in front of my line of sight, he bent down and picked up a small object that was yellow and shiny. His face turned to joy as he examined his 'find.' - I could just barely make it out to be a gold wedding band.

He turned his head and saw that I was observing him and gave me a look of fear as if I was in a position of power and he was caught doing something illicit.

"Nice find," I called out to him, to his visible surprise. He clenched his hand around the ring and looked at me.

He opened his hand and approached me and replied "My Lucky day." then paused and his smile disappeared.

"I cannot sell this as I am not legally documented here in France." he began.

"I'd like you to have this." he then proceeded to hold my hand, open it and deposit the ring in my hand. I looked at it closely, seeing what appeared to be a jeweller's mark on the inside of the ring with a 14-carat designation, typical of wedding bands. Hefting the ring, I calculated it to weigh about just under a half ounce.

Not believing the generosity of this man, I tried to protest, explaining to him that he would surely find a pawn shop or even a person in a coffee shop or other public venue that he could try to sell this ring too.

He assured me that his lucky day would have to be my lucky day because society would never allow a person such as himself to dispose of this find for anything near its true worth, and showing me the non-verbal signals of total defeat, hunched shoulders, head hung low, he proceeded to walk away.

"Wait!" I cried out after him, pulling out my wallet, I withdrew a 20 Euro note and handed it to him. "For Lunch," I told him.

He came back calmly and took the note gratefully, and looking into my still open wallet, asked me if he could count on my generosity for a warm meal for dinner as well. I looked at the contents of my wallet and thought about this poor unfortunate man, who most likely lived on the very edge of society, and I took out a 50 Euro note and put it in the palm of his hand, on top of the first note.

"For Lunch and Dinner, mon ami," I replied.

He became emotional, and an actual tear streamed down his cheek. Smiling, he thanked me profusely and melted away into the crowd.

I finished my coffee and walked back into the train station and made my way to the nearest uniformed policeman. Explaining the story to the policeman, I told him I'd like to turn in the ring in case the owner turned up looking for it and innocently asked him if the process of reporting the find would take long because I had a train to catch.

It was when I observed the grin on the face of the policeman that I realised what had happened.

"Monsieur, you have been scammed." the policeman informed me, trying to keep his face professional. "It's fake, it's not even metal," he explained, not even bothering to take a close look at the ring I was holding.

I felt sick. I had rewarded the dishevelled man for his generosity and willingness to give up his treasure only to realise that he played me.

Thinking back to this book and the stories that Mark and I had researched together, I smiled.

"Well played, monsieur...well played."

# FINAL THOUGHTS – MARK RODGER

As humans, it's in our genes to want what the other guy has, which is why "Envy" and "Greed" are included among the Seven Deadly Sins. In life, there are the hard-workers, the dedicated, and the people that just want to make a better life for themselves or others. Amongst them are people that want what they have, they just want to get it more easily and without working for it. Maybe they do work for it, even if it's just a different sort of work ethic.

I have always had an interest in scams, rip-offs and confidence games, and the people that have the guts to run them. It would be easy to say that such people are criminals, evil-minded and predatory on normal, kind-hearted and honest folks. I'm not so sure it's quite like that. There's a duality at play that I can appreciate.

We can admire a character like Robin Hood, happily robbing the rich to give to the poor while forgetting that stealing is wrong. Is he really a hero? Shouldn't we have been rooting for the Sheriff to lock him up? Somehow the idea of the charming rogue flouting authority and getting away with the money with it can be appreciated, so much so that we conveniently ignore that he was sticking arrows into people as he did it.

There is a part of us that wants to be fooled, and we admire ingenuity and smarts. Audiences still clap wildly for stage magicians and illusionists; we laud them for fooling us and making us believe what we know to be impossible. Only in a magic show could an entire audience be wildly enthusiastic about the prospect of watching a woman get sawn in half or drowned in a glass booth and pay extra for seats up front. We know that we're being misled, that we are being deceived, and line up to watch it happen and be part of it. Sometimes we can admire being tricked.

When I was 15, I went to an annual fair where I grew up, complete with the travelling circus performers, carnival rides and tent games like whack-a-mole and guess-your-weight. There's always an element of Barnum and Bailey in the air, and even though most people realise that it's harder than it looks to knock down cans or throw rings on the tops of bottles, they still get lured in and try to win the giant stuffed animals. There's always such delicious smells in the air, like popcorn and candied apples that stupefy and entice us to try just one more time to win the game and beat the odds.

On this particular summer day, there was a tent with bright yellow and red awnings and large, billowing flags that I had never seen before. Outside, there was a carnival barker with a cane and top hat telling the passing tourists that for only $1 they would see something rare and unusual – an anomaly that the visitor would never forget; that had to be seen to be believed. Inside, he promised – was a Man-Eating Chicken that has recently been discovered and caged for viewing and examination. People were lining up to go in, and I watched dozens of people leaving out the rear entrance, all shaking their heads in disbelief at what they had seen. Sold, I enthusiastically handed over the money and joined the throng to go in. Customers were separated from the exhibit by a metal mesh, which was presumably for their protection as they filed past the small stage, which was lit by a spotlight. Seated squarely at a table was a man with an over-sized napkin tucked under his chin, happily eating a bucket of fried chicken. In less than a minute I emerged again out into, the sunlight at the back of the tent and became one of the people I had just seen, shaking my head in disbelief. I couldn't help but admire it, and all these years later it was worth the price of admission. It makes me chuckle still at how easily I was taken in.

A decade later, I learned the lesson again in a different way. Half a world away, I was travelling in the south of Italy and stopped in a typical market area, filled with a mixture of the usual flea market stalls and small local shops dependent on the tourist trade. I was leaving in a couple of days for home, and like most pleasure travellers became focused on acquiring those last minute souvenirs for family and friends. It's a strange tradition, buying ashtrays and keychains for loved ones as a remembrance of a trip that they didn't take. I was probably looking for ashtrays in particular.

One shop I went into had a certain appeal. Smaller than some of the others, I remember there was a little brass bell that chimed happily as I creaked open the door and there were shelves crammed with curios that gave me the impression that I was in an antique store, and not likely to find postcards or ashtrays. I noticed the thick smell of lacquered wood and the complete absence of any other customers. At the back, there was a kindly-looking old lady type who would have reminded anyone of their grandmother, dressed in conservative black with her hair in a bun and wearing an apron. I thought she might be in her seventies, and she greeted me in thickly accented English, coming right up to ask me about the heat outside, where I was from and how I enjoyed the food in Italy. She thought I might have been with an American tour group from one of the buses parked outside, as they generally stopped in the area as they ferried travellers north to Rome, but seemed very interested to find out that I was from Canada and heading home shortly.

As I browsed, she chatted happily and followed me along and asked about Canadian winters, my family and asked if I was going to bring my mother anything. Apparently, it was always particularly important for travelling Italians to bring something home for their mothers, and she helpfully pointed out a few items of interest that she thought might suit her, but nothing, in particular, captured my interest on her shelves. After completing a circuit of her store, I was angling for the exit when she stopped me to say that she had something that might be the very special gift

I was looking for, not on display as she hadn't thought of what she might sell it for yet. From beneath her counter, she produced the most colourful ashtray, fashioned like a turtle and covered in little fragments of shells like a mosaic. It was hand-made, and not manufactured as I was expecting. There was turquoise, shades of red, blue and orange and twin slivers of silver that made up the eyes.

It was a wonderful little piece, and as I felt its weight, I wondered if it might be stone. The shopkeeper explained this was one of the many little things that her grandfather had dug up over the decades; apparently, he had been an amateur treasure hunter in his youth. She said that she thought it must be old, but couldn't say for certain of course. Charmed, I offered her less than we eventually settled on and I paid almost 70 Euros for it. It felt strange to haggle over money with such a helpful grandmotherly type. As I counted out the bills to her hand, she said that although she wasn't certain that she actually wanted to sell the turtle at all, she felt better that it was going to be a memoir of my travels for my mother all the way across the Atlantic in Canada. As a final friendly gesture, she helpfully offered to gift-wrap it for me and after disappearing with it into the back emerged a few minutes later with a wrapped and stylish little box, topped with a perfect little bow. I left the store feeling satisfied and excited that I had a great "how I got this for you" story.

A few days later when I returned to Canada and unpacked I went through the usual routine of the traveller, inspecting everything as I lay it out on my bed. I decided to have another look at the turtle, and after carefully unwrapping it, I was appalled to see that inside that nice little box was nothing more than a fist-sized rock. I had been taken.

# The End

A great deal of research and love went into the creation of this book, we would appreciate feedback, both positive and constructive, from our readers and invite you to review our work on Goodreads or any other similar book review forums.

Made in the USA
Coppell, TX
12 December 2020

44365724R00144